D0437535

Fantasies of the Library

Library of Congress Cataloging-in-Publication Data

Names: Springer, Anna-Sophie, editor. | Turpin, Etienne, 1980- editor.
Title: Fantasies of the library / edited by Anna-Sophie Springer and Etienne Turpin.
Description: Cambridge, MA : The MIT Press, [2016]
Identifiers: LCCN 2016010260 | ISBN 9780262035200 (hardcover : alk. paper)
Subjects: LCSH: Libraries--Philosophy. | Libraries in art.
Classification: LCC Z721 .F36 2016 | DDC 027.001--dc23 LC record available at https://lccn.loc.gov/2016010260

Fantasies of the Library

Edited by
Anna-Sophie Springer
& Etienne Turpin

Dear Reader,

Having picked up our book *Fantasies of the Library*, you're likely curious about just what fantasies you'll find here. Like libraries, there are many kinds of fantasies, so which should you expect to encounter? We have set out to create a book about the library as a curatorial space—a physical knowledge infrastructure organized as the veritable index of cultural and epistemological orders and aspirations, but also as a virtual domain of possibilities for other orders, logics, and dispositions. Whether the *fantasy* is best characterized by the ambition for a correct and complete ordering of knowledge, or by the attempt to remake inherited orders in pursuit of less authoritarian styles of learning, we leave up to you to decide. But, before you begin, we want to share with you a few remarks about the book itself.

Originally published in a first edition under the same title, *Fantasies* began as a part of the *intercalations: paginated exhibition* series, which we edited together as members of the SYNAPSE International Curators' Network at the Haus der Kulturen der Welt in Berlin. The project is conceived as a curatorial-editorial space to both host and critically reflect on contemporary exhibition-making practices and their modes of knowledge co-production, while also enabling explorations of the book as a form of exhibition architecture in relation to other aesthetic practices in the Anthropocene. How does this agenda relate to the library as both a curatorial space and a technology for thinking?

In 1931, the Indian mathematician and librarian Shiyali Ramamrita Ranganathan published *Five Laws of Library Science* as a concise guide for librarians: 1) Books are for use; 2) Every reader, her book; 3) Every book, its reader; 4) Save the time of the reader; 5) The library is a growing organism. We like these heuristics because they make it clear that the library is a fundamentally relational space—with connections and affinities distributed among the librarians and the library users, the books themselves, the interior space of the collection and the world outside its walls. While libraries have traditionally been considered systems to aggregate and access knowledge, they are no less infrastructures for thought in need of special care. We explore the library as a system and an infrastructure, but also as a curatorial space enabling custodianship, solidarity, exploration, and the promiscuity of affective and conceptual constellations. Especially influenced by ideas of praxis and change—Ranganathan's first and fifth laws—*Fantasies* is a book about the ways we organize and archive culture and scholarship, and how these assemblages shape, in turn, the ways we think, read, and write.

Change has become so ubiquitous that in our present situation we can easily fail to think about the speed and consequence of even epochal shifts. When the concept of the Anthropocene can be rendered as just another theme for the perpetuation of biennales and conferences, it is hard to grasp the value of overcoming binaries. What's really at stake when transgressing these alleged divides between nature and culture, human and non-human, if their politics and history aren't taken seriously? We became more interested in the problems of organization and discipline. Must order and creativity be considered oppositional practices? Isn't the overvalued estimation of creativity, especially in the register of the curatorial, often just a permissive password that allows for loose associations and the absence of rigorous engagement under the neoliberal big tent? Fantasies are not—as is so often imagined—the product of spontaneous invention; they require care, cultivation, and discipline to truly disrupt their systems of containment.

The productive unruliness of book collections and the potent "spirit of freedom" which Virginia Woolf associates with the practice of reading are taken up in Anna-Sophie Springer's essay, "Melancholies of the Paginated Mind," and her visual essay, "Reading Rooms Reading Machines." Discussing medieval examples, Aby Warburg's Hamburg reading room, and André Malraux's imaginary museum, as well as the vulnerable but steadfast library of the Occupy movement, and a mobile library initiated by the Asia Art Archive, *inter alia* Springer maps how the rigid organization of knowledge can be renegotiated in pursuit of more experimental connections, arrangements, and display.

The first of the three interviews featured in *Fantasies* also deals with the desire for a singular arrangements among the collection. In conversation with Erin Kissane, Megan Shaw Prelinger and Rick Prelinger of the Prelinger Library speak of their love for getting lost while exploring a library's open shelves, and how they developed their very own taxonomic imaginary for organizing their stacks. Additional reflections on the role of cultural memory and the archive are unfolded throughout our conversation with Hammad Nasar from the Asia Art Archive. The question at the center of this interview is how to inject the archive with positions from the perceived geographical or intellectual margins in order to re-calibrate hierarchies and unleash possible future trajectories by re-evaluating, in the same movement, how we read these entangled histories.

While producing these *Fantasies*, we encountered the artistic work of Andrew Norman Wilson; his series *ScanOps* (2012–14), which conjures a spectre of cultural appropriation, is intercalated throughout this volume. "ScanOps" is the internal referent for Google's book scanning facilities in California; the series collects the errata which occur during the digitization process that produces Google Books. The images of book pages defaced by accidental stains, smears, and dirty rubber gloves are a profound reminder of the physical labor that generates the allegedly universal cognitive access to content owned and further monetized by Google. But the erratic magenta fingers also implicate the proprietary software used by Google to quickly detect these conspicuous pink digits and thereby delete any trace of the labor and laborers producing their digital investments. They reveal the processes required to *format* knowledge—as such, they also issue an uncanny reminder about the formidable difficulty of (ever) fully erasing its history of production.

This fantasy library shares concerns and aggregated labors, a construction site full of temptations, shifting alliances, and the reproduction of reproductions. Perhaps this is because we're old enough to remember going to *the library*. When we wanted to do research, or to learn, we went to *the library*. If the physical journey to a physical space has been replaced for so many readers by *searching*—"I search therefore I scroll," as our friend Geraldine Juarez says—the curatorial work of the librarian has also been largely replaced by proprietary search algorithms that monetize every single query, amassing a fortune with which to acquire ever more content. In this way, it's not just the librarian who has been digitized and privatized, but the public relationship with the collection as well. As Wilson noted in his 2013 interview with Laurel Ptak, "The workers compose part of the photographic apparatus, which in a broad sense includes not only the machinery but the social systems in which photography operates. The anonymous workers, Google founders Sergey Brin and Larry Page, the pink 'finger condoms,' infrared cameras, the auto-correction software, the capital required to fund the project, the ink on my rag-paper prints, me—we're all part of it." While preparing this book, Google's parent corporation, Alphabet, became the most valuable company in the world, with an estimated worth of $520 billion USD. Within this vast accumulation, we do not know the precise value of Google Books; nevertheless, *we're all part of it*. Juarez, while describing Google's colonial aspirations, remarks, "Organizing information is never innocent. … Colonization without the archive is a purely military affair." Without promoting culture online, Google would appear as it really is—an engine searching for ever new ways to maximize its profit. Certainly, we cannot leave what a library should do to the world's wealthiest corporation.

In the second half of the book, the conversations therefore turn to digital publishing, open access, online sharing, and text collecting. You will find a letter originally written earlier this year by the artist and co-director of K. Verlag, Charles Stankievech, as legal support of the non-profit internet library platform Arg.org, which is currently facing a copyright infringement lawsuit in Canada. While elaborating the ways in which Arg.org activates a community of independent researchers, Stankievech's epistle is also an urgent plea for the democratization and free accessibility of information, which must not be turned into just another fantasy of monetization through paywalls and exorbitant subscription fees. The open ethics of the book are also explored in our interview with the philosopher Joanna Zylinska, who describes the contours of the book as a series of platforms, enterprises, and collaborations that marshal a multi-faceted technology for negotiating the Anthropocene. Driven by a lithe combination of intellectual rigor and a "just try" mentality, Zylinska argues for greater creativity and open access in academic publishing, while also returning the conversation to the codex as a decidedly human technology of thought and encounter.

Before we conclude, we would like to thank the community which made this book possible. We thank all the contributors and artists for sharing these various bibliomanic fantasies. We are grateful to Bernd Scherer, Kirsten Einfeldt, and Daniela Wolf from the Haus der Kulturen der Welt for founding and coordinating the SYNAPSE International Curators' Network and inviting us to develop *intercalations*. The first edition of the book would not have existed without the generous support of the Schering Stiftung and we are here especially indebted to Heike Catherina Mertens for her ongoing mentorship and advice. Regarding the intricacies of the book-as-exhibition, we thank K. Verlag co-director Charles Stankievech for his support and invaluable criticism; Lucas Freeman for transcribing and copy-editing our interviews; Martin Hager and Jeffrey Malecki for their meticulous attention as copy editors; and Louis Steven and Miriam Greiter for administrative support. We are also grateful to our generous interlocutors, including A Public Library, Fiona Geuß, Fotini Lazaridou-Hatzigoga, Caleb Waldorf, Ho Tzu Nyen, Vincent Normand, The Showroom, Emily Pethick, Joanna Zylinska, Lindsay Bremner, Printed Matter, Keith Gray, David Senior, Julia van Haaften, Ruangrupa, Dian Ina, Farah Wardani, PrintRoom, Karin de Jong, Sara Giannini, Jason Groves, Jennifer Cazenave, and John Paul Ricco. A very special thank you to our designer, Katharina Tauer, for her incredible dedication, commitment, and openness to experiment with us while creating this work together. Last but not least, we are grateful to Roger Conover from The MIT Press for his enthusiasm about publishing this new edition.

We won't keep you any longer—please enjoy these *Fantasies* as they connect, conspire, and intercalate among your own.

Anna-Sophie Springer & Etienne Turpin
Jakarta, February 2016

Melancholies of the Paginated Mind:

The Library as Curatorial Space

Anna-Sophie Springer

The imaginary is not formed in opposition to reality as its denial or compensation; it grows among signs, from book to book, in the interstice of repetitions and commentaries; it is born and takes shape in the interval between books. It is a phenomenon of the library.

— Michel Foucault, "Fantasia of the Library," 1967

Melancholia is the fundamental tonality of functional systems, of current systems of simulation, of programming and information. Melancholia is the inherent quality of the mode of the disappearance of meaning, of the mode of the volatilization of meaning in operational systems. And we are all melancholic.

— Jean Baudrillard, "Simulacra and Simulation," 1981

The Library as Map

Megan Shaw Prelinger (M S P)
& Rick Prelinger (R P) in
conversation with Erin Kissane (E K)

The Prelinger Library is a private reference library in downtown San Francisco. Founded in 2004 its holdings currently comprise more than 50,000 publications of various genera. The majority of items in the collection are present in hard-copy form, and books, magazines, and other printed matter can be pulled from the long, tall bookshelves in the warmly lit, high-ceilinged room fronted with working tables. However, since a growing number of the library's materials have been digitized for the online platform The Internet Archive—and are hence living on the server stacks at *Archive.org*—even remote visitors can access the Prelinger Library. Here anyone can look up and download files such as the official guide to the Chicago *World's Fair*, books like *Safely on We Go* (on the prevention of accidents) or *Landology De Luxe* (an early twentieth-century textbook on farmland development), and several volumes of *Scribner's Magazine*.

Inspired by Aby Warburg's "law of the good neighbor" the Prelinger Library's organization does not follow conventional classification systems such as the Dewey Decimal System. Instead it was custom-designed by Megan Shaw Prelinger in a way that would allow visitors to browse and encounter titles by accident or, better yet, by good fortune. Furthermore, somewhat evoking the shifts in magnitudes at play in Charles and Ray Eames's *Powers of Ten* (1977) the shelves' contents are arranged according to a geospatial model departing from the local— material specifically originating from or dealing with San Francisco—and ending with the cosmic—where books on both outer space and science fiction are combined with the more ethereal realms of math, religion, and philosophy.

When editor and writer Erin Kissane first visited the Prelinger Library she immediately realized how easy it was to get lost for hours and hours among the stacks, dipping into unusual books, and leafing through boxes of 'zines. The online library, entwined with the physical collection in subject and type, lives conceptually very near to the Prelinger Archives, which includes thousands of digitized advertising, educational, industrial, and amateur films. Between research jags, screenings, and editorial work on their many concurrent projects, the Prelingers spoke with Kissane about the nature and fate of libraries and archives in an increasingly digital age.[1]

EK	MSP
When I first learned about the Prelinger Library, one thing that stopped me in my tracks was the idea of a collection arranged for serendipity. Can you introduce the arrangement of the physical library?	The library's arrangement scheme was designed in response to several conditions: First, the collection is unique to our combined areas of particular interest. It has never tried to be a general-interest research collection. Second, therefore, the

From Book to Books

In the final scene of Alain Resnais's meditative short film on the French National Library of Paris, *Toute la mémoire du monde* (1956), the narrator's voiceover highlights the crucial shift of value that occurs as soon as a specific book has been selected and requested from storage by an individual user:

> And now the book marches on toward an imaginary boundary / More significant in its life than passing through the looking glass / It's no longer the same book / Before, it was part of a universal, abstract, indifferent memory, where all books are equal / ... / Here it's been picked out, preferred over others / Here it's indispensable to its reader, torn from its galaxy / ... / This and other universes offer up their keys to us / ... / simply because these readers / Each working on their slice of universal memory / Will have laid the fragments of a single secret end to an end...[1]

Echoing the Bergsonian concept of actualization, this emphasis on selection and constellation, however idiosyncratic, is at the heart of curatorial thought and practice as one method of making meaning, however esoteric. And, as will become clear, the pulsation of the library—the very push and pull between axioms of organization and subjective propositions—plays a specifically powerful role in the following essay, both formally and conceptually.

1   Alain Resnais, *Toute la mémoire du monde* (F 1956), B/W, 21 min (included in the DVD Alain Resnais, *Last Year at Marienbad* (F 1961), B/W, 94 min, *The Criterion Collection*).

library did not really fit the taxonomic systems of either the Library of Congress or Dewey Decimal. For instance: Art and politics? Handmade films? Nature-culture interface? The history of the demonization of youth in society? These are just a few of our subject areas that are not clearly articulated in pre-existing taxonomic systems.

Third, for us—for myself in particular—the process of research is inseparable from the physical process of exploration of the world. In my experience, creative and intellectual work flows from physical engagement with the landscape. There are literal manifestations of this, such as the discovery of forgotten places and the collection of forgotten literature from the shelves of a rural shop. More intangibly, the processes of walking, hiking, or taking a road trip are useful activities for developing new ideas or thinking through puzzles.

Given these conditions, it became self-evident to organize the library's shelves in a way that harmonizes with the process of exploration: Where are you when you begin each exploration? What parts of the world do you engage with first in the process of exploration? Where do you "end"? Etc. The result is a landscape-based, geospatial arrangement system. This system, in outline, "starts" where the library is, in San Francisco, and "ends" in outer space. Its rough structure moves from place-based subjects to the made worlds of art, media, and culture, to abstracts like society and philosophy, to space exploration.

For example, the first row progresses from the San Francisco section eastward, across the North American landscape to the Atlantic, where it makes a transition to general landscape-based subjects such as natural history, nature-culture interface, agriculture, rural life, and extractive resource industries.

The associative subject flow itself is designed to facilitate serendipity, and

serendipity is enhanced by the practice of creative juxtaposition of materials within subject sections. Government documents are shelved near modern monographs that interpret them, and satirical histories are shelved next to serious ones. Subject-matter fiction is interspersed amongst nonfiction, and trade literature can sometimes stand for a whole topic. (Our run of *National Safety News* is the whole "safety" section.)

The library is divided into two major parts: the open bookshelves, and the boxed ephemera collection. The geospatial arrangement system is duplicated in both places, but only the bookshelves offer surprising juxtapositions. The flow of subjects within the geospatial arrangement system is described in some detail on our site http://www.prelingerlibrary.org /home/collection.

EK

The browsing experience of physical bookshelves—and even of the web—is so absorbing, but our digital archives and libraries still struggle to serve browsers and wanderers. How can we create absorbing browsing experiences in formal collections of digital works?

MSP

A lot of people have thought more than we have about the future of the digital bookshelf. You probably know about them: The David Rumsey Map Collection is set up in Second Life for avatars to physically browse the collection. The Institute for the Future of the Book is working on models of digital bookshelves. What I really see being needed is a way for query-based search to mimic the kinds of associative links that are formed by shelving different kinds of literature next to one another on a shelf. What if, when you typed in a search term, your result was a color-coded cloud of virtual book covers?

4

In European culture, the history of using books as the material or site of art goes back at least as far as Stéphane Mallarmé in the nineteenth century. It can easily be traced much further back, to times before the printing press, to include early experiments in combining text, images, and binding techniques in the Middle Ages and even before.[2] According to Johanna Drucker, a scholar of artists' books, one of the reasons why the book has not lost its thematic and material vitality, despite our all-encompassing digital reality, is the "tension between the seeming simplicity of that conventional form and the unlimited complexity produced through the relation of elements to each other in a finite arrangement."[3] With the right balance of skill and imagination, the book provides a virtually inexhaustible space for formal and conceptual expression. Within art history, the broad international spectrum of artists' books, bookworks, magazines, and even small publishing imprints, has been extensively researched and received substantial scholarly attention. However, from the perspective of an emerging curatorial discourse, the conceptual richness of the book as medium can be further explored. There are at least two ways to pursue this curatorial agenda in relation to the book. One potential vector would examine the role of individual publications as adjacent or primary exhibition spaces, where single exemplary books and their interiors could be examined as if they were miniature galleries. By parsing the differences and correlations between the objecthood and content of books within practices

2   It seems important to mention in this context that the world's oldest, entirely preserved printed book is from the East: a Chinese version of the Buddhist *Diamond Sutra*, which was found in a cave in northwest China. It is a scroll dated to the year 868 AD, and today it is held in the British Library in London: www.bl.uk/onlinegallery/sacredtexts/diamondsutra.html.

3   Johanna Drucker, *The Century of Artists' Books* (New York: Granary Books, 2007), 359.

In the cloud, covers highlighted in one color would represent the straight response to your search query. Jackets highlighted in other colors, floating behind them, could follow any of hundreds of other associations. Perhaps you could select half a dozen supplemental associative searches from a list before you begin your search. Then you see a layer behind your straight result that's composed of satires, or other works by the same author, or public records that relate to your search term—or every work that's cited within a given book's bibliography! Features like those would inject intense excitement into digital search.

RP

Allow for chance and serendipity. Let people get lost in the library. Make it very simple to "pull a book off the shelf_ and open it up." There is so little you can do with a mouse and trackpad. It's a shame that the richness of today's screens seems to be accompanied by such a constrained toolbox for human-machine interaction.

EK

You two have been working as archivists and librarians during the shift from entirely tangible archives to archives both tangible and electronic. How has your work changed, or not changed?

RP

The most dramatic effect for us has been the propagation of our collections to a mass audience. It's hard to be precise, but it's safe to say our films have had at least seventy million views. That's pretty unprecedented for a historical moving-image archive. And while we can't know the number of derivative works made from our archival film collection, our images are ubiquitous and have made their way into just about every kind of image-bearing medium.

We've also found that the turn toward digital has a de-familiarizing effect on analog materials. In the library, we've discovered that print has become a privileged medium whose allure seems to grow greater as books recede from the everyday sphere. So while the world enacts the end of print and the onset of bit-based book simulations, it simultaneously celebrates print as a special kind of experience. This is a bit uncanny, like simultaneously being vegan and carnivore, and I think we're a few years away from sorting out how we really feel about books. But the fascination is real—we track it by reading the faces of our library visitors, especially the younger ones, who are entranced by high shelves of books, every one of which they are invited to pull down and open.

EK

I remember you once told me that kids and teenagers were some of your most fascinated visitors. Why is that?

MSP

Part of that is situational, because a lot of people who teach at area colleges and universities bring classes in to tour the library and do projects. So that creates a proportion of college-age library users who become part of our core community. Many college-age library visitors return again to do projects, even long after they've left school. Over the years, this accumulation of college students and young post-college people has resulted in us having a core community that is generally young.

But part of the answer is also how we're positioned within the community: We are a local workshop, not an institution. We serve tea, and we encourage photography and scanning and any other form of non-destructive appropriation. That kind of environment is very natural to people in the millennial generation and people who have

such as the artistic, editorial, design, and curatorial, one could gain valuable insights about the latter as the youngest and most hybrid of these practices in a dynamic field of production.[4] A second trajectory, ours, would begin to consider collections of books and the exterior space that contains them—the library—in order to explore the potential for curatorial reflection. If the book is traditionally seen as the preferred medium for private consumption and research, and the gallery is understood as the space for public exhibition and performance, the library—as the public place of reading—is thus a hybrid site for *performing the book*. Furthermore, if the librarian is seen as a rational agent responsible for providing access to book collections for research and reading, and the reader is the one who comes and goes from outside, the curatorial agent of the library inhabits the interstice between librarian and reader, working on improbable exchanges that might excite, provoke, seduce, or otherwise perturb the paginated mind.

As the curator moves among alternative spaces and the power of the image-as-reproduction continues to grow, the library collection remains an underexplored platform where the curator may operate site-specifically to co-construct thought-provoking reinterpretations at various levels: the texts and reproduced and reproducible images, the collection (its history and function), and even the institutional architecture. Libraries are akin to the archive and the museum in that all three types of institution exist in order to collect, research, and

4   Recently, however, a few reconsiderations have emerged, such as Beatrice von Bismarck, "Exhibitions, Agents, Attention: In the Spaces of Ruscha's Books," in *Reading Ed Ruscha*, ed. Yilmaz Dziewior (Cologne: Walther König, 2012), 66–75; Lisa Le Feuvre and Fraser Muggeridge, "Books and Sculpture," *HMI Essays on Sculpture* 95 (Summer 2013): 5–36; Anna-Sophie Springer, "Volumes: The Book as Exhibition," *C Magazine* 116 (Winter 2012): 36–44.

grown up during the resurgence of craft and DIY spaces.

The third part of that phenomenon is that there aren't as many older books in wide circulation as there were in previous decades. Some teens have grown up in homes where they absorb cultural knowledge entirely through digital channels. We get high school groups as well as college students. Some of these teenaged visitors have never really held an "old" book before. I've heard teenagers scream with enthusiasm that they are being "allowed" to touch and hold an "old" book. And smell it. They become extremely tactile and extremely involved during their explorations of the library. This is the most illuminating part of having a lot of young people in our library's community. It has shown us that 3-D objects, rather than having been de-valued in the digital age are if anything being re-valued.

E K

Megan, you've said that part of the project of the library is to "collapse the working distinction" between analog and digital, and you've also talked about the ways in which the integration of the two can "animate" a collection, allowing it to serve different audiences in different ways. Can you say more about that?

M S P

The library project is an experiment in collapsing some of the working dualities between analog and digital modes of access. Our collection has been partially sponsored for digitization by the Internet Archive, to the net result that about five percent of our materials are freely available online, in PDF, e-reader, and text-searchable formats. Hundreds of thousands of downloads of books and documents have been facilitated through this system. The digital collection serves people all over the world, and it serves them around the clock.

Access to the physical library is limited to our opening hours, yet library visitors have access to twenty times more material than those using just the digital books from our collection. And those visitors have a physical browsing environment to facilitate their access. Often, online access to the digital collection inspires a subsequent, deep visit to the brick-and-mortar library. This is one way that digital access animates the analog shelves.

Digital access events usually rely on query-based retrieval, while visitors to the physical library are immersed in a physical, tactile environment of discovery. Visitors are able to use the process of browsing the shelves as a mode of discovery, and then retrieve some materials they find online, and "have" a copy in digital format. This turns the shelves into a "finding aid" for digital materials, inverting the more familiar experience of using a computer to discover a book and then subsequently getting access to a physical copy.

We find that people can use the library in both ways, and get completely different results from their respective discovery processes. This yields a creative tension between analog and digital modes of discovery.

This sounds like I'm emphasizing the differences between analog and digital modes of access, and I am, but with the intent of showing that they can be so different from one another that they complement and do not compete with each other. The physical library offers not just a single irreproducible experience—browsing—but thousands of irreproducible experiences of browsing-based discovery. Looked at in this way, my point is to reframe what's too often a competition between digital access and analog browsing. I see them as very different, and most effective when they are combined and dovetailed.

make accessible objects that carry information in material culture. As repositories of collective memory they are all traditionally based on rationalistic and objective principles of organization, which, in the case of the library, manifest themselves in a rigid order derived through themes, numbers, and alphabetical sequences. Especially with regard to archives and museums, it has become standard practice to invite independent agents (typically those referred to as "artists") to engage with existing collections in radical or novel ways, with the hope of reanimating the holdings according to contemporary agendas or alternate histories and epistemologies, all while refurbishing the attraction of aging institutions and soliciting new audiences. Considering projects such as Fred Wilson's groundbreaking *Mining the Museum* (1992) at the Maryland Historical Society in Baltimore, it is clear that, at least on some occasions, these creative and critical reconsiderations are capable of actualizing powerful and transformative ruptures within dominant cultural narratives.[5] Yet, while museums typically house "original objects" (specimens of natural history, artifacts, and artworks) and attempt to mediate the relation to their collections of objects in some more or less authentic way, the library—at least since Gutenberg, if not longer—is a space of mass-production and reproduction leading to slightly different conditions. Among these, perhaps one of the most fundamental is that the library's primary function privileges use over display and presentation, whereas museums and archives normally store objects and information only *after* the time of their utility has expired.

5   Fred Wilson is an American artist who reinterpreted the heritage collection of the US
     state of Maryland by questioning its inherent racism and critically highlighting the
     gaps and omissions in representing African and Native American culture in this official
     narrative. The intervention was highly praised and became a seminal model for alternative curatorial approaches to traditional collections made by artists and curators alike.

In the future we'd like to progress even further beyond these distinctions, and replicate some of the physical browsing process in a digital bookshelf environment, but that would require large-scale digitization.

Even so, however, not all materials are good candidates for digitization: many eighteenth- and nineteenth-century materials, artists' books, copyrighted materials, periodicals with tipped-in, stapled-in, and glued-in layered pages, and very large format materials are just a few kinds of texts that come to mind that are hard, if not impossible, to offer in digital format. Materials for which digital access represents a qualitatively secondary form of access. So there will always be irreproducible advantages to both modes of access—hence a creative tension rather than a competition.

E K
Rick, you've said elsewhere that the US in particular is very "media rich," but also very careless with media, and inclined to throw a lot of it away. What are we throwing out?

R P
Here in the US we produce media on an astonishing scale. Even before the age of personal video production à la YouTube and outside the near-infinite realm of home movies, large and small producers made tens of thousands of training, promotional, and instructional films each year. After video effectively supplanted film in the 1980s, the number of corporate, institutional, and government videos produced became impossible to count. These were usually small productions made for specific purposes at specific times; longevity wasn't on the minds of their producers, and the works disappeared when their makers or sponsors lost interest or ceased business. It may be easier

to understand their ephemerality by thinking of why and how we shoot video with our phones today—ritual recording of everyday experience, a message to a friend or intimate, or an entry in what amounts to an unstructured digital diary without pretensions of permanence. Most of these videos won't last, either.

E K
What do we lose if they don't survive?

R P
While most archivists feel that every film and video is unique and every frame is precious, it's not easy to define what it means to lose some. Retaining many instantiations of similar occurrences (a million Christmases, a hundred auto sales training films) strengthens the corpus of human documentation, but confuses it at the same time, and we can never really know what it means not to have saved everything.

I am intrigued when I'm asked how I feel about our inability to save everything, as if this should make me sad. Why are we so focused on completism? The idea that a complete archive of human activity and experience constitutes a good thing isn't by any means a new idea, but it gained currency a few years back when technological advances convinced many of us that collecting and preserving everything was possible. Then, just as in "feature bloat," possibility turned into desirability. The data firehose has convinced us that selection is impossible, and we assume that decisions as to what we save will be determined purely by our IT capabilities. That cultural and social criteria (not to mention power differentials) might actively determine what we preserve—well, that's turned into an "oldskool" idea.

Just as alternative curatorial modes and methodologies have become popular for museums, book-themed exhibitions in gallery spaces have become a rather widespread phenomenon. Exhibitions such as *The Feverish Library* (2012), a group exhibition held at Petzel Gallery in New York, have presented artworks that address the multifaceted and longstanding cultural significance of books, especially by considering their recent attractiveness and shifted general value in the face of digital technology. The exhibition *The Whole Earth* (2013), held at the Haus der Kulturen der Welt in Berlin, is another example of a recent show that essentially unfolded from a publication—but also, at least partly, performed itself as a book (or textbook). These examples, among the many others that could be cited, illustrate that both individual books and constellations of and about books are not at all foreign to curatorial work. In fact, the use of literature as a starting point for curatorial concepts and storytelling is a classic strategy. But what about the library?

In literature, the locale of the library is of indisputable significance, operating both as a cradle from which narrative worlds unfold and as a metaphor for the world at large. "The library was a special, embryonic place where a person could sit with the vibration of lives off the walls, all around him,"[6] writes Ray Bradbury, who began his literary career as a young man by working inside public libraries, and in whose dystopian novel, *Fahrenheit 451*, books are both fiercely condemned and passionately cherished for their intellectual infinity. But the ungraspable, boundless dimension of the library has been

6   Ray Bradbury, "Libraries, the Love of My Life," in *Logotopia: The Library in Architecture, Art and the Imagination*, ed. Sascha Hastings and Esther E. Shipman (Cambridge, ON: Cambridge Galleries, 2008), 60.

EK

From outside the archive world, it looks as though there is a split between archivists who carefully select things to preserve, and those scrambling to save everything. It sounds like you're closer to the former group.

MSP

We are careful selectors, nowhere near the "save everything" end of the continuum. What's most interesting to us is to build our own very specific collection, and in doing so model ways of collection-building that could be useful to other people. We want to embody the idea that everyone can be their own archivist. If more people carefully chose a collection of evidence to save, then there would be less of a need for people to save everything. Libraries like ours can be built by anyone, anywhere. We do have a particular collecting strategy, but we are just two people.

RP

We absolutely cannot save everything. And we shouldn't. Loss is formative. Absence is necessary to truly under-stand presence. I would never advocate the intentional destruction of cultural materials, which is quite often an act of aggression. On the other hand, many of the emergent historical discourses of the past forty years were spurred by the sense that materials were sparse, lost, or destroyed. I'm thinking of working-class history, African-American history, women's history. A perceived lack of traditional historical evidence caused scholars and, critically, interested lay people to look harder, dig deeper, and search in unanticipated places. And now these histories flourish.

EK

How do you prioritize what should be saved in your own collections?

RP

Our library acquisition and retention policy is, frankly, subjective and unwritten. As for film, we collect all home movies shot in North America or by North Americans abroad. We seek to build a complete visual history of North America and its inhabitants in the twentieth century that's at least as complete as we can, using home movies.

MSP

We are really interested in ephemeral evidence: What kind of picture of history is revealed by forgotten literature? What's been left out of the canon of memory? What's of visual interest? What's been overlooked within the public domain? We use questions like these as a guide, and then we look closely at what's being discarded by libraries and collectors. With this strategy it's possible to strike some really rich veins. (We also buy materials some-times, and receive many donations from like-minded community members.)

We are working toward a composite picture of American history, formed by a multitude of these rich veins of ephemeral evidence: trade literature, government documents, illustrated technical periodicals, 'zines, small-press books, maps, pamphlet literature— each of these types of literature holds hidden riches. For that reason we are more focused on such ephemera than on "books," per se.

EK

I know the Prelinger Library is very much a working library, and that you both have a lot going on. What were some of your more recent projects?

MSP

I am writing a book that's a visual history of electronics, *Inside the Machine: Art and Invention in the Age of Electronics*.

made most explicit in Jorge Luis Borges's famous description: "the universe (which others call the Library)."[7] The traditional custodian of the library is, of course, the librarian (focused more on practical matters of acquisition and access and less on the aesthetics of display), and books might seem to primarily address readers and writers rather than viewers, but libraries comprise massive collections of useful objects that merge aesthetic materiality, idea-based profundity, and a profusion of images. So, in addition to the librarian who builds a rationalistic system of connections and the user who accesses this structure to create something that will ultimately live outside the library (and sometimes return to it again later), should the "universe" of the library not also be complimented, or challenged, by new curatorial practices that affect the pre-existing structures in a more creative way from within? This idea becomes even more worthwhile when we recognize, reminded perhaps by Bradbury's own biographical statement, that books are in themselves already more than mere containers of information; they are also modes of connectivity and interrelation, making the library a meta-book containing illimitable intertextual elements.[8] By focusing on the curatorial space of the library, we can gain further insight into how the practice of the curatorial is being shaped in this expanded field.

7   Jorge Luis Borges, "The Library of Babel," in *Collected Fictions,* trans. Andrew Hurley (New York: Penguin, 1998), 112.

8   Though the term intertextuality goes back to Julia Kristeva, Roland Barthes more fully expressed the concept that a text does not contain its meaning statically but is produced by the reader in the process of reading, and as a complex entanglement of subjective evocations immediately connected to innumerable other texts. Roland Barthes, "From Work to Text," in *Image-Music-Text,* trans. Stephen Heath (New York: Noonday Press, 1977), 155–64; Walter Benjamin reflected repeatedly on the interplay between reading, writing, and the library in texts such as "The Work of Art in the Age of Mechanical Reproduction" and "Unpacking My

It is based on a study of industrial litera-ture in which commercial artists depicted electronics components using visual language inspired by modernism. The book is forthcoming from W.W. Norton in 2015. Together, Rick and I were artists-in-residence at the Exploratorium, San Francisco's science museum, and we built an exhibit called the *Observatory Library* that is about observing San Francisco Bay, both its built and natural environment. The exhibit has several parts, a book collection, moving-image loops, and a series of historical atlases that we wrote using collected and digitized ephemera, both from our own library and from other repositories. The Observatory Library was opened in April 2013.

RP

My recent project is *No More Road Trips?*, a feature-length documentary film about the past and future of motor travel in America. There is reason to think we are traveling less and may drive less in the future. Are precarity, the high cost of fuel, the increasing age of new drivers, and the slowdown in car ownership significant factors in keeping us off the road? Is the frontier that we once reached by long drives beginning to close in? Will localism triumph? The form of the film is a dream road trip built through home movies without sound. It is the audience who make the sound-track, talking throughout the movie while facilitated by an MC. The film premiered in May 2013.

EK

In closing, could you introduce us to an artifact—or set of them—in your collection? Something you have been particularly interested in recently?

MSP

We are excited about our relatively recent collection of Civilian Conserva-tion Corps camp newsletters.[2] These were mimeographed newsletters written and produced by CCC members to inform and entertain one another. The newsletters were produced all across the country between 1933–43. They are filled with quirky language, local humor, and a rich record of everyday life as experienced by CCC workers.

I have also been very focused, myself, on the *Proceedings of the Institute of Electrical and Electronics Engineers*. That is an amazing journal, the *Proc IEEE*. In the 1960s it featured amazing modern art about electronics on its covers, and it ran articles with historical and social relevance supple-menting its mostly technical articles. It is still the leading engineering tech-nical journal, but it had a "golden era" between 1962 and 1974 that I am immersed in right now.

1   The original version of this interview first appeared in the online magazine *Contents*, issue no. 5, January 2013: http://contentsmagazine.com/articles /the-library-as-a-map. For the re-issue in *Fantasies of the Library* the text was slightly edited and received a new introduction.

2   The Civilian Conservation Corps (CCC) was a public works relief program that operated from 1933 to 1942 in the United States for unemployed, unmarried men from relief families as part of the New Deal. Originally for young men aged 18–23, it was eventu-ally expanded to young men aged 17–28. Robert Fechner was the head of the agency. It was a major part of President Franklin D. Roosevelt's New Deal that provided unskilled manual labor jobs related to the conservation and development of natural resources in rural lands owned by federal, state, and local governments. See http://en.wikipedia.org/wiki/Civilian _Conservation_Corps.

Legere and βιβλιοθήκη:
The Library as Idea and Space

It felt like being inside an enormous brain. Imagine being totally surrounded by those shelves, full of books in their compartments, ladders all over the place, all those book stands and library tables piled high with catalogs and bibliographies, the concentrate of all knowledge, don't you know, and not one sensible book to read, only books about books.

— Robert Musil, *The Man Without Qualities*, 1940

Etymologically linked to vocabulary such as the Latin *legere*, which can mean both "collecting" and "reading," and the Greek *bibliothēkē*, or "bookcase," the library—from Robert Musil and Virginia Woolf to Jorge Luis Borges and Walter Benjamin to Alberto Manguel and Moyra Davey—is inhabited as a space of tension between chaos and order, a space of collecting information of and about life and the universe in an attempt to make sense of it through organization, reading, commentary, and interpretation. This establishes the library both as archetype and prototype for storing knowledge, literally a device of historiography itself. The most famous ancient library that was designed as such was, of course, the mytho-historical Library of Alexandria. From around 300 BC until the beginning of its destruction with the Roman imperial takeover under Julius Caesar, the Library of Alexandria was the principal workplace for international scholarship. In light of this discussion of the curatorial, it is worth noting that this classical library was in fact incorporated into a larger complex known as the *Mouseion*, or House of the Muses, which formed

Library: A Talk about Book Collecting," in which he writes: "Of all the ways of acquiring books, writing them oneself is regarded as the most praiseworthy method" (61). Both essays in *Walter Benjamin: Illuminations*, ed. Hannah Arendt, trans. Harry Zohn (New York: Schocken Books, 1968), 217–51 and 59–67.

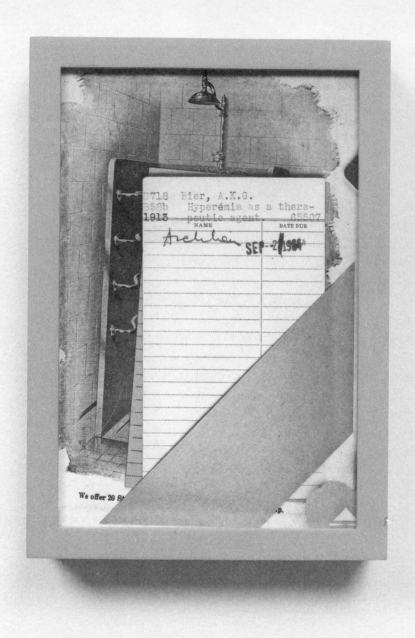

Andrew Norman Wilson, *Hypermia as a Therepeutic Agent – 251*, 2014. Courtesy of the artist.

a multidisciplinary study center similar to a university (etymologically, it is the source of the modern word "museum"[9]). In his erudite meditation on libraries, Alberto Manguel makes the observation that in terms of a conception of the world, the Library of Alexandria and the Tower of Babel are direct opposites. While the tower represents the "belief in the unity of the universe," the library instead embodies an understanding that the world is made up of innumerable different voices that, if somehow *collected and read*, would "address the whole of creation" through their very singularity and yet, as an ensemble, could never become static.[10] Expanding Manguel's comparison, it is interesting to consider the two architectures in relation to concepts of dispersal and containment. In the moment of its destruction fragments of the Tower are violently and irretrievably flung out in all directions across the Earth, whereas the Library derives its meaning as a space of proximity for gathering together such fragments. "Books are not dispersed but assembled," as Georges Perec asserts in "The Art and Manner of Arranging One's Books."[11] If we consider that the Library's assumed founder, King Ptolemy I, used to send missives around the world pleading for "every kind of book by every kind of author,"[12] the myth of an all-embracing

9   For an in-depth history of the Library of Alexandria, see Roy MacLeod, ed., *The Library of Alexandria: Centre of Learning in the Ancient World* (New York. I.D. Tauris, 2005). On the history of cultural loss and the mass destruction of libraries, see James Raven, ed., *Lost Libraries: The Destruction of Great Book Collections since Antiquity* (New York and London: Palgrave Macmillan, 2004).

10 "The Tower of Babel collapsed in the prehistory of storytelling; the Library of Alexandria rose when stories took on the shape of books, and strove to find a syntax that would lend each word, each tablet, each scroll its illuminating and necessary place." Alberto Manguel, *The Library at Night* (New Haven and London: Yale University Press, 2006), 23–4.

11 Georges Perec, "The Art and Manner of Arranging One's Books" (1978), in *Species of Spaces and Other Places*, ed. and trans. John Sturrock (London: Penguin Books, 1997), 150.

12 Manguel, *The Library at Night*, 22; with additional references to Luciano Canfora, *La biblioteca scomparsa* (Palermo: Sellerio Editore, 1987).

Andrew Norman Wilson: ScanOps (2012–14)

Grappling with the Anthropocene thesis can foster a sensitivity to the various relations between humanity and technology. Among the many theses about what is currently shaping our lives on this planet is also the idea that, by competing for accumulation and progress, humans have often become more isolated socially, less in direct contact with other beings, and therefore lonelier than in any previous epoch. Countless hours of lived time are spent on and with computer-machines; to a vast extent, human contact has become mediated through devices, media, apps, and social networks; we tell each other that our interpersonal communication suffers from "email fatigue." Coming uncannily close to Spike Jonze's recent science fiction film *Her* (2013), in which the protagonist falls in love with his operating system, social immediacy now sees technology as its inter-face. What such descriptions overlook, however, is that there is a form of anonymous human presence that continues to reside inside of seemingly disembodied digital processes. And, where could the evidence of this presence be more haunting than in the old-fashioned and—quite happily—solitary realm of the book?

The reader-as-exhibition-viewer will encounter a selection of art-works from Andrew Norman Wilson's series *ScanOps* (2012–14) intercalated throughout *Fantasies of the Library*. The series consist

library evokes yet another Old Testament story, that of Noah's Ark as a repository for living specimens of every existing species. While the Ark was built to survive the Great Flood, the Library of Alexandria—ancient repository of memory for the paginated world—was destroyed by flames.

The intrinsic connection between the library and grand cultural narratives still perpetuates today; reflecting such great ambitions, the Bibliotheca Alexandrina was, for instance, recently rebuilt and declared a "window" between contemporary Egypt and the rest of the world.[13] In the context of Occidental history, however, libraries are especially symbolic of a particular Enlightenment sensibility. Poignantly addressed by Victor Hugo in *The Hunchback of Notre Dame*, libraries became the new cathedrals of cities when science and the attendant desire to disseminate knowledge replaced the religious impetus of previous generations. Stories were no longer told primarily through clerical art and architecture but were instead translated, multiplied, and circulated through printed books. In Hugo's novel, this idea is summarized in the phrase "*Ceci tuera cela*" ["this will kill that"]—a provocative exaggeration, though the printing press by no means did away with architecture, just as the digital turn has not replaced printed matter. What is true, however, is that the ethos of the public library (in contrast to private, monastic, or other specialized and restricted libraries) continues to be intimately connected to democratic ideals of equality and free access to knowledge

---

13 The institution was inaugurated in 2002 as a UNESCO project; the complex was designed by the Norwegian/American architectural firm Snøhetta Arkitektur og Landskap. The library has the capacity for eight million volumes and aims to be a center both for traditional media and digital materials, though whether the shelves will ever be filled to capacity is uncertain due to financial and other constraints.

of prints made from pages found in Google Books that reveal a variety of unintended glimpses betraying the physical tasks employed in their digitization. Once a book shows up in the browser window, the transformation from physical library to electronic archive might appear quite effortless, like some act of invisible magic. But scanning millions of books requires Fordist tasks of repetitive labor such as the turning of pages and the operating of machines for manual scanning. Sometimes the proof of these modes of hand-made production sneaks into a book because a reproduction is blurred by an uncontrolled bodily movement or a worker's hand was caught out of place. These slippages of material labor are what interest Wilson; by making the productive labor tangible as aesthetic accidents and paginated ruptures, he reminds us of the human presence inscribed in the immaterial processes of the age of digital reproduction.

All images courtesy of the artist.

and culture. Such libraries are usually non-profit spaces, which provide citizens with material and immaterial goods and media that would otherwise have to be purchased. Therefore, one of the many ways in which the library contributes to society is by converting marketable goods into public goods. The potential of the library for making things public is furthermore reflected in its paradoxical reality as an intellectual meeting place: based on intellectual and communal values, it also lends a public platform to otherwise fundamentally private—whether mental or cerebral—activities like reading and thinking, thus connecting it with ideals such as free speech and the freedom of expression. The library is thus both a political economy and an intellectual space. In a recent essay, media studies and library scholar Shannon Mattern has emphasized this notion by discussing several recent initiatives of so-called "little libraries," that is, community or artistic endeavors of setting up alternative "para-libraries" in urban public spaces. The author addresses the role and use of such initiatives in light of the institution of the public library as their general model. While she critically questions a number of these projects as potentially counter-productive, especially when trying to hold governments accountable for their responsibilities as providers of sufficient public space, as one strong, positive example she describes the guerilla libraries of the Occupy movement. Mattern stresses their antithetical but complimentary role in relation to online media and communication, arguing that these politicized street libraries draw their importance from the occupation of physical public space, while symbolizing the "right to knowledge" for the 99 percent. Furthermore, their collections are said to reflect and express the ideologies and intellectual culture upon which the

Andrew Norman Wilson, *The Inland Printer – 152*, 2014. Courtesy of the artist.

movement is based.[14] As a phenomenon also observed recently in the major protests in Turkey—when publishing houses and readers came together to build a street library in Istanbul's Gezi Park—and which has intensified through the news about several violent attacks on the Bibliotheca Alexandrina during the political upheavals in Egypt in August 2013, it is crucial to understand how books and libraries are embraced in political struggles for freedom.

In This Madhouse of Books

In order to allow for our subjectivities to unfold by selecting and engaging with whatever book-fragment we request from their archival holdings (and then reanimating these fragments through individualized and intertextual reading processes), public libraries have typically been standardized in order to administer the retrieval of books in an ordered form. There are several different library classification systems currently in use, such as the Library of Congress Classification (LCC) for academic libraries (mostly in the English-speaking world), and several more varied approaches in Germany. The most widely accepted library ordering system is the Dewey Decimal Classification Scheme (DDC), originally invented in the 1870s by the American librarian and rationalist Melvil Dewey (1851–1931). Applied in general public libraries to this day, it laid the

14 See Shannon Mattern, "Marginalia: Little Libraries in the Urban Margins," *Design Observer*, 5 May 2012, www.placesjournal.org/article/marginalia-little-libraries -in-the-urban-margins. On publishing houses setting up camp at Gezi Park in the summer of 2013, see "Publishing Houses to Unite in Gezi Park to Distribute Major Resistance Material: Books," *Hürriyet Daily News*, 4 June 2013, http:// hurriyetdailynews.com/Default.aspx?pageID=238&nID=48234&NewsCatID=341.

Andrew Norman Wilson, *North Of England Institute of Mining Engineers. Transactions, Volume 9 – 306*, 2014. Courtesy of the artist.

foundation for the LCC and other academic classification systems. One of the reasons the DDC has survived for so long is that its mathematical sequences can be broken down infinitely in order to add new categories to the nine conceptual "classes" that Dewey initially conceived. Despite its relative flexibility and ubiquity, Dewey's invention has been criticized for reflecting a culturally narrow interpretation of objectivity, privileging white, Anglo-Saxon, and Christian worldviews, and thereby excluding a range of alternative perspectives on human knowledge.[15] But the imposition of a particular standpoint is not unique to the DDC. Since it is usually possible to assign one book to multiple categories at once, any chosen library system—whether in a private, "individual bureaucracy" (Georges Perec) of free associations, or in a public context—will reflect particular assumptions, while operating through a combination of various classificatory modes. Library classification systems are rational structures inherently motivated by a "fear of being engulfed by this mass of words,"[16] and yet, even if they are powerful enough to suppress this fear, in so doing they proliferate other limits, cracks, and misguided trajectories.

"How do you find your way in this madhouse of books?" asks Robert Musil's General Stumm of the librarian. The following reasoning suffices to inform the General: "The secret of a good librarian is that he never reads anything more of the

---

15 See Melvil Dewey, *A Classification and Subject Index for Cataloguing and Arranging the Books and Pamphlets of a Library* (Amherst, MA: 1876), www.gutenberg.org /files/12513/12513-h/12513-h.htm; "Decimal Classification Beginnings," *Library Journal* 45 (February 1920). Dewey biographer Wayne A. Wiegand called for a critical analysis of the DDC's approach to categorization based on the writings of Michel Foucault and Pierre Bourdieu, in Wiegand, "The 'Amherst Method': The Origins of the Dewey Decimal Classification Scheme," *Libraries & Culture* 33, no. 2 (Spring 1998): 175–94.

16 Resnais, *Toute la mémoire du monde*, 02:35.

Andrew Norman Wilson, *Motor Age – 7*, 2014. Courtesy of the artist.

literature in his charge than the titles and the tables of contents. 'Anyone who lets himself go and starts reading a book is lost as a librarian!' ... 'He's bound to lose perspective!'"[17] As a caricature of the librarian, the passage nevertheless highlights the act of cataloging as the core aim of the rationalizing work in the library; the result of this painstaking process is, of course, the catalog. A means for listing and indexing the complete holdings of a library, the catalog is the central nervous system of the library's organization. It serves as the primary interface to library books. In the past, the catalog was actually an assembly of index cards or a continuously expanding series of bound volumes; nowadays it is usually an online database that can be accessed remotely.

In its essential role as a list of items in a collection, the library catalog bears some resemblance to the early exhibition catalog, which originated as a simple list to carry as a reference while viewing the artworks in an exhibition. In fact, it was not until the mid-twentieth century that exhibition catalogs evolved into aesthetic and critical compendiums more ambitious in scope, size, and scholarship.[18] One important figure in this evolution was the Swedish art collector and curator Pontus Hultén (1924–2006), who first directed the Moderna Museet in Stockholm, and then moved on to establish and develop the Centre Pompidou in Paris in the 1970s and early 1980s. Influenced by Marcel Duchamp's writing and the radicality of his *La Boîte Verte* (1931), in the 1950s Hultén began to understand exhibition catalogs as "art experiments" that ought to

17   Robert Musil, *The Man Without Qualities, Vol. 1.*, trans. Sophie Wilkins (New York: Vintage Books, 1996), 503.
18   See Pnina Wentz, "Writing about Art Exhibition Catalogues: A Literature Review," in *Exploring Science in Museums*, ed. Susan Pearce (London: The Athlone Press, 1996), 172–77.

Andrew Norman Wilson, *The Inland Printer – 164*, 2012. Courtesy of the artist.

correspond to their respective museum exhibitions but relay them beyond the institution's walls. Exemplary of the curator-editor, he was often described as such: "Hultén is a passionate reader and curator, who creatively processes his knowledge for himself and others in exhibitions and libraries. He uses literature and libraries in their most fundamental role: by liberating the immaterial, spiritual energy stored in them and transforming it into something new and idiosyncratic."[19] A profuse reading practice is thus leveraged as a means to reinvent the mode and display of the re-read collection.

Regarding its aim to be a comprehensive index, the library catalog also shares its ambition with the encyclopedia. In the second half of the eighteenth century, Denis Diderot edited what is considered the first modern encyclopedia, the visual dictionary *Encyclopédie, ou Dictionnaire raisonné des sciences, des arts et des métiers*. Like our contemporary *Wikipedia*, it was written by way of collective effort, and like the aforementioned Library of Alexandria, it is an example of a utopian project to collect and represent all of human knowledge. The absurdity of any such endeavor is at the center of Borges's seminal story, "The Library of Babel" (1941). For Borges, it is above all the library's monstrous catalog that expresses a sense of perversion. For, by containing all of its errors and their corrections, the catalog's role is that of a palimpsest inevitably turning sense into nonsense. Borges thus accentuates the relationship between order and entropy, portraying the library as a nightmare and the apotheosis of paradoxical irrationality.

19   See Lutz Jahre, "Zur Geschichte des Ausstellungskataloges am Beispiel der Publikationen von Pontus Hulten," in *Das Gedruckte Museum von Pontus Hulten*, ed. Lutz Jahre (Ostfildern: Cantz, 1996), 31. All translations in the text are the author's own unless otherwise indicated.

Andrew Norman Wilson, *The Works Of Nicholas Machiavelli – 530*, 2014.
Courtesy of the artist.

From In-Between the Covers:
Erudite Dreams

Even though arrangements such as alphabetical and numerical systems—and still more so, modern keyword cross-referencing—already bring individual items into cognitive relation with each other, it is ultimately only the subjective and diverse desire from within a collective usership that can complete the library in its mission and meaning. In contrast to Musil's literary figure General Stumm, who in Chapter 100 of *The Man Without Qualities* "invades" the National Library in Vienna with the rather passive, yet also conventional, expectation to find "a kind of timetable that would enable [him] to make connections among all kinds of ideas in every direction,"[20] it is Walter Benjamin, in his essay "Unpacking My Library," who highlights the relationship between objectivity and subjectivity as a core mechanism of the library. Showing that connections are not inherently present or preordained, as General Stumm seems to think, but must be made, Benjamin writes: "[C]ollectors are the physiognomists of the world of objects—turn[ing] into interpreters of fate ... To renew the old world."[21] As actualizations of the past, all interpretations affect both the present and the future.

One such collector-author is at the center of an essay by Michel Foucault, "Fantasia of the Library." Foucault's "protagonist" is Gustave Flaubert (1821–1880), who spent nearly

---

20 Musil, *The Man Without Qualities*, 502; German original: "etwas wie von Eisenbahnfahrplänen, die es gestatten müssen, zwischen den Gedanken jede beliebige Verbindung und jeden Anschluß herzustellen." Musil, *Der Mann ohne Eigenschaften*, Vol. 1. (Reinbek b. Hamburg: Rowohlt Verlag, 1978), 461.
21 Walter Benjamin, "Unpacking My Library," 60–1.

Intensive Geographies of the Archive

Hammad Nasar (H N) in conversation
with Anna-Sophie Springer (A S)
& Etienne Turpin (E T)

Among the fantasies of the library frequently entangled in contemporary curatorial discourse and its manifold expressions, desire is a strong archival impulse. We see it as an especially valuable trajectory for examining collections of printed matter and the new modes of cataloging, accessing, and disseminating work, which characterize contemporary archival practices. How does the archive function as a means for new work while enabling meaningful open access to unconsidered histories? How can the reformation of the collection transform art practice? What are the consequences of rethinking the archive? These questions animate our thinking and provide the reader-as-exhibition-viewer with a series of departure points for reimagining encounters among the various manifestations of the archive, their geographies, latent opportunities, and structural limitations. In this interview, conducted in Jakarta in July 2014 following his lecture at the Jakarta Art Fair by Hammad Nasar, Head of Research and Programmes at Asia Art Archive in Hong Kong, editors Anna-Sophie Springer and Etienne Turpin, together with Hammad, consider the role of the archive as a relay for possible practices of art that rearticulate chronologies, geographies, centers of production, and means of dissemination. The following edited version of this conversation suggests some of the institutional, operative, and strategic questions at stake in contemporary collections, their reevaluation, and modes of access and circulation.

E T

You have described your work as intent on recalibrating the art world away from its global centers, like New York and London, toward more neglected geographies, particularly South Asia. Before we turn to questions of the archive in contemporary practice, can we begin with the geographical orientation of your work?

H N

The orientating metaphor I used at Green Cardamom was the ocean.[1] Do you know Peter Fend's work? In a work based on water flow in the world's oceans he demonstrates how the world's water systems are centered on the Indian Ocean. Peter suggests that if you look carefully at the water flows and currents, the Indian Ocean is a sort of centrifugal hole that is driving everything. This geographic orientation is even reflected in the command structure of the Pentagon—Central Command is in the Indian Ocean, while the Atlantic and Pacific are, in that framing, peripheral. This militaristic application is, perhaps, slightly disturbing, but I thought it was very interesting too. That's why I've often found his drawings an effective way to talk about Green Cardamom's attempts to inject an international that comes from the Indian Ocean into the Atlantic Ocean-driven art world. The idea was to displace, or at least complicate, thirty years writing his novel *La Tentation de saint Antoine* (1874).[22] In the text, which was first published as an afterword to the German translation of the book (1980), Foucault focuses on how Flaubert's writing is built upon and intrinsically made up of a re-composition of previous records, such as paintings, religious narratives, and, especially, the world of books: the library. Foucault sees everywhere the proliferation of the book (and also The Book)—itself an important trope for *The Temptation*—calling Flaubert's literary work the "book of books" and describes how it "recovers other books; ... hides and displays them and ... causes them to glitter and disappear,"[23] which through a sense of fluidity and movement evokes certain ideas about the curatorial as a dynamic field eliciting a "constellational condition."[24] In his essay, Foucault makes another key point that elucidates a pre-condition for understanding curatorial agency as a practice that provokes meaningful shifts through imaginative connections between existing materials and knowledge. In fact, Foucault contends that it was Flaubert who opened the way for a new form of subjectivity in the nineteenth century, one in which the imaginary is experienced as arising less from nature or nocturnal dreams and more from the repositories of accumulated knowledge.[25] The dreamlike state actuated by reading practices

22   B.F. Bart, *Flaubert* (Syracuse: Syracuse University Press, 1967), 581.
23   Michel Foucault, "Fantasia of the Library," in *Language, Counter-Memory, Practice: Selected Essays and Interviews*, ed. Donald Bouchard, trans. Donald Bouchard and Sherry Simon (Ithaca: Cornell University Press, 1977), 92.
24   See the descriptions of the curatorial in the conversation between Irit Rogoff and Beatrice von Bismarck: "Curating / Curatorial," in *Cultures of the Curatorial*, eds. Beatrice von Bismarck, Jörn Schafaff and Thomas Weski (Berlin: Sternberg Press, 2012), 21–38, especially 24, 28, and 31.
25   Foucault, "Fantasia of the Library," 90–1: "its treasures lie dormant in documents ... it derives from words spoken in the past, exact recensions, the amassing of

what people think of as an idea of the "international." When I was studying at Goldsmiths, my approach was to consistently make a point of having referents who were not French philosophers. For example, I was reading Eqbal Ahmad, the political scientist, writer, and activist who first came to prominence while working with the National Liberation Front in Algeria, and I'd base my arguments on his texts and interviews. When I spoke, I'd see professors frantically writing notes because they didn't know who I was talking about. And I would say: "Oh, you don't know him? Edward Said dedicated *Culture and Imperialism* to him. Said called him his political mentor. You don't know this guy?" It became a project about provoking people to open up to what they didn't know about the so-called "international."

In a way, I think a fundamental problem that a lot of curators and intellectuals face, particularly in the large institutions that build curricula, collections, or narratives, is that it is very easy to build a narrative around the twenty, thirty, or forty people who know about particular subjects or histories. But what happens when you try to scale that literacy up to 400 or even 4,000 people? The standard model—the conventional mode of narrative building—simply falls short. The foundation holding up these exclusive edifices begins to shake. A few months ago, I was moderating a panel in Hong Kong for a Museum Summit, and I spoke with museum directors in Europe and North America whose institutions have now begun to address the contemporary outside Euro-America, but who are still not addressing the Modernist collections they are known for; they are not asking questions about the histories that they authored. So, I tried to explain that they were looking into the future, projecting into the future, but without reevaluating the histories they wrote. The response I got was a bit shocking: "That

history has been written. Other people can write their own histories. We're looking to the future. The time is now; no looking back." So, a fundamental question for me is: "What are you doing to question your own collection?" No matter how interesting the future projects are, if the answer is "nothing," I think there is a serious problem.

AS

So, despite your evasion of French philosophers, your approach seems to have strong affinities with Deleuze and Guattari's concept of cartography as a transversal practice that undermines the definition of territories rather than producing stable objects. This might be considered a method particularly suited to the Anthropocene.

HN

Exactly. There is also the need to rethink the history and development of chronologies and timelines. I'm not native to the art world or to art history, as you may have gathered. Relatively late in my life, when I started working on histories of art at Goldsmiths—and, you know of course that Goldsmiths is a very trendy institution for theory—the first thing that struck me was that there was no place for chronology. So, on the one hand, that seems kind of cool, but I was curious about why this was excluded from the discourse. There is the model of chronology as a kind of text, but the timeline is also a tool for historical orientation. These are two very different things. At the Asia Art Archive (AAA), we are now trying to think about and develop chronologies that can serve as tools. Let's make no bones about it: we could only come to this point because of all the materials that have been collected, and all the networks that have been built. We can't get around that. It might be seductive to think that you could move straight into becomes a methodological and transformative bridge. To illustrate his point about making "art within the archive,"[26] Foucault portrays Saint Anthony—whom Hieronymus Bosch, Brueghel the Younger, and others had already depicted as absorbed in a heavy book and surrounded by the conjurings of improbable, hellish creatures—as a direct reflection of Flaubert's own "visionary experience," itself gained "from the black and white surface of printed signs, ... words spoken in the past ... and the reproductions of reproductions."[27] In the fantasia of the library, the reader-writer Flaubert resembles Saint Anthony, as both characters are surrounded by ever-mutating temptations springing forth from their paginated imaginations. If Foucault's analysis could be further condensed, we would find, again, the accentuation of the library as a space of intertextuality, creation, un-creation, and recreation:

> In writing *The Temptation*, Flaubert produced the first literary work whose exclusive domain is that of books; following Flaubert, Mallarmé is able to write *Le Livre* and modern literature is activated—Joyce, Roussel, Kafka, Pound, Borges. ... *The Temptation* was the first literary work to comprehend the greenish institutions where books are accumulated and where the slow and incontrovertible vegetation of learning quietly proliferates. Flaubert is to the library what Manet is to the museum.[28]

minute facts, monuments reproduced to infinitesimal fragments, and the reproductions of reproductions."

26   Ibid., 92.
27   Ibid., 90–1.
28   Ibid., 92; with Gertrude Stein (1874–1946) and Virginia Woolf (1882–1941), however, the list is extended to include modernist women writers. For a

an instrument-building project, or an operational chronology, but the archive must be made. Where are your roots? Where are you anchored? Where can you extend? If you have no connection to history, there is no way you can extend to the future. We see that we have some points of contact, important histories; we're thinking about how we can refashion this information to produce tools and instruments, rather than canons or texts. This goes back to your earlier remark that texts have a limited scope, whereas instruments and tools can be extended and shared beyond the limits of the text. We're beginning to think about our mobile library, and the various programs we run around it, as a way of both ceding control and enabling our collaborators to do more. For example, as part of our Sri Lanka mobile library project, we managed to get some funding from the FfAI (Foundation for Art Initiatives) with which our local partner—a publishing company called Raking Leaves—was able to set up the Sri Lanka Archive for Art, Architecture, and Design.[2] The name alone tells you that their archive has a different shape and focus than the AAA, but we're not in the business of cloning ourselves. The idea is to tap into these energies and support them.

A S

So, do you think the institutions act as a kind a basecamp? How does the AAA approach the work of forming a new institution?

H N

The institution question is an interesting one to me, so let me start with a personal reflection and then work back to it. For part of my misspent youth I worked as a management consultant, and part of my area of focus was organizational design. The first time I ever really travelled through Asia, I was helping one of the big banks redesign their wholesale banking organization. That kind of work involved all sorts of different things, but it was fundamentally about organizing how people will work. And these organization structures need to change over time; so how do we build in the capacity to flex the design to fit different stages in the evolution of an organization? These structures send out very important signals, internally and externally, about the identity of an organization. At the AAA, we are also going through this assessment and adjustment of how we evolve. And this is reflected in many things, for example, on our website. One of our major projects next year is to upgrade our website in order to make it more open. We are also looking at finding people to bring onto our advisory board to challenge us on how open we actually are, not just in terms of technology, but in terms of ownership, rights, and how we balance our responsibilities and our goal of access. There will always be a lot of negotiation and critique, and that's okay ... but I am drifting away from your question.

Coming back to institutions and our organizational structure, if you go to the research page on our website—which, as I mentioned, we are in the midst of overhauling—there is a description of how many people we have, and how many researchers we have had in different places. Basically, it's a display, or a stage for a kind of cartography. We're mapping, and we're saying: look, we've done Manila, we've done Seoul, Mumbai, Tokyo, etc. So, there is a kind of will to authority that is connected to the presentation of how many researchers we have, and where we have worked, which is projected to viewers and readers through our website. It can be read as though we are trying to make our institution an authority. Don't get me wrong, I think this a

Like the Library of Alexandria, for Foucault, Flaubert's "library is on fire,"[29] and thereby resonates with another energetic-literary space: Borges's "feverish Library" whose "volumes constantly threaten to transmogrify into others, so that they affirm all things, deny all things, and confound and confuse all things, like some mad and hallucinating deity."[30]

The Law of the Good Neighbor

The rearrangement of archival information in order to compose new adjacencies and meanings is an intersectional activity where the work of writing, editing, and curating become difficult to distinguish. If only as a difference in degree, the curatorial nonetheless tends more decidedly towards incorporating spatial and material articulations, as well as temporal factors related to sequencing, installing, and de-installing. A library whose fragments are reassembled in a writing project like that of Flaubert—or a hundred years later, by way of Kathy Acker[31]—and then held in a codex-bound book is typically organized in a linear manner, producing a work that can be reinserted back into the cultural archive from were it was

consideration of intertextuality in relation to working from inside the library, see also Nikolaus Wegmann, *Bücherlabyrinthe: Suchen und Finden im alexandrinischen Zeitalter* (Cologne: Böhlau Verlag, 2000).

29   Foucault, "Fantasia of the Library," 92.

30   Borges, "The Library of Babel," 117.

31   The feminist writer Kathy Acker (1947–1997) famously appropriated, cut up, and rewrote works and passages by the foremost male literary canon such as Cervantes, Dickens, Faulkner, Genet, Hawthorne, Stevenson, Twain, Rimbaud, and others. One of her many means to critique the patriarchy was to replace the male protagonists with female characters, which she for instance did in *Don Quixote: Which Was a Dream* (New York: Grove Press, 1986).

necessary step in the development of the organization; you can't just sit in Hong Kong and say, "Yes, we will tell you about Korea," without having relevant sources and materials, without having done the work of being present. But, the Archive is now nearly fifteen years old. So, one of the first things that we did when I joined—which I don't think was unexpected—was to question whether or not this model of research is sustainable, given the kind of organizational spirit that we have already and to which we aspire. My colleagues get annoyed when I say this, but our research structure was close to that of a multinational bank, with a branch office and a branch manager. Or, even further back and even more problematically, one can make comparisons with all those colonial efforts like the East India Company. You have an agent who negotiates and acts as the funnel through which you see into the region being represented. For very practical reasons, we started off with these "representative" roles, but given what we are and what we are trying to achieve, this model is no longer appropriate. Even on purely logistical grounds, it is not sustainable. We simply cannot have representatives in all the 108 nations that make up Asia. Even if we did, I think there is a problem with that kind of relationship. So, we are busy rethinking the relationship we have with nations and regions. We are trying to develop a node-and-network organizational structure rather than a central/branch office structure.

Now, that's not to say that there's no value in having dedicated resources! But still, we are refashioning the way we staff projects. The staffing doesn't need to come only from us. Every operation doesn't need to be completely guided by us. We can have rough guides. For example, in Cambodia there was an influential organization called Reyum that is no longer around, but did important work.

We have been struggling to figure out how to shape a project to work with them. Reyum can be thought of as a set of impulses or agendas. One of their agendas was the desire to explore what the "contemporary" could be in Cambodia. And what its relationship would be to traditional folk practices. Some of what they do is related to exhibitions, but a lot isn't. So, what we have started doing is to reach out to a friendly, engaged academic deeply invested in these histories who can help us deal with the requisite constellation of people and practices. She can be our guide. We can support a pilot project with some initial funding, provide a platform for Reyum's work to be shared, but not directly manage the staffing or production processes, which remain autonomous within a negotiated structure.

If we step back and ask ourselves what we can do—the things that the Getty and the Guggenheim, the Australian National University, and the Power Institute, to name a few institutions invested in different ways in the region, can't do, won't do, or are not interested in doing—I'm sure the list we'd end up with would be very long. But one of the things that we can do is to throw some grit into the smooth functioning of the global circuits— the art fairs and biennales, even the so-called "critical" circuits—because these all function in a parallel way, no matter what people want to tell themselves. For AAA, it is important to slow these circuits down in whatever way we can. Let's be honest though, we are only thirty-five people. In any case, we are trying to question this hard line between the past and the contemporary, and ask what is allowed or accepted in each circuit. If you smuggle things in from one circuit to another, you disrupt it, even if only slightly, or itinerantly.

born. Meanwhile, a curatorial engagement with the library has the capacity to elicit additional physical modes of reassembly, perhaps not unlike the short scene in Lars von Trier's *Melancholia* (2011), where a manic Justine rearranges the books displayed in her sister's study. Arranged on a shelf, a series of art books are opened to certain spreads, held in place by thin, horizontal rubber bands, displaying a selection of constructivist and cubist twentieth-century paintings. The emotionally disheveled Justine exchanges this cold constellation of geometric shapes for a series of allegorical paintings by Brueghel, Millais, Caravaggio, and others, creating not only a referential mirror for the many pictorial scenes quoted and restaged in the film, but also an especially striking visual referent for her own despair as excluded from a contemporary culture of perpetual enjoyment.

Within the history of the library, there is one particular example for which the "shifting and re-shifting"[32] of the books on the shelves has been absolutely crucial to its character: the unconventional library of Aby Warburg (1866–1929), begun in Hamburg in 1901 and persisting today in London as the Warburg Institute associated with the University of London.[33] The interplay of symbolism, gestural language, psychology, and meaning as exercised by von Trier's character Justine was

32 Fritz Saxl, "The History of Warburg's Library," in *Aby Warburg: An Intellectual Biography*, ed. Ernst Gombrich (London: The Warburg Institute, 1970), 327.
33 The ongoing dispute about sovereignty and responsibility between the University of London and the Warburg Institute was put to a stop only recently, in early November 2014, when it was decided in a court ruling that the University was not entitled to dissolve the Institute's collection into its various other libraries, but on the contrary was obliged to secure and support the Institute's future existence as an independent site of research; see the Warburg Institute's press statement following the ruling from 6 November 2014: http://warburg.sas.ac.uk/home/news/high-court-ruling.

In a way, you are fuelling the fire as much as slowing it down. The lateral connectivity and modes of affinity that you help establish are absorbed so quickly; the art market is stalking behind the Archive for a new constellation to subsume. Of course, I don't believe that you can hide anything— obscurity and obfuscation aren't necessarily any more effective at defying the market; in fact, often the opposite is true—but I am curious about how the work of the Archive is appropriated.

HN

Well, I think you're right, but there's nothing we can do! If I turn the question around on you, I could ask about your work with Twitter, because it is exactly the same thing. Your Twitter feed project—your appropriation of the platform and the data it produces—is going to be read by developers and turned into a means for accumulation as well.[3] So, yes, our projects are also going to be read and used by galleries and museums. I joined shortly after AAA launched a major digitization project on the Filipino artist, teacher, and curator Roberto Chabet, and I came into much collective soul-searching within the organization about what had happened, which was basically that, following the launch, there were a number of Chabet projects at galleries, museums, and art fairs. Around that time, a major UK institution said to me that they wanted to look at Chabet; when I asked how they came across the work in the first place, they said, "we saw it at Frieze and all the images said Asia Art Archive." We all thought that we had just unleashed another monster into the global circuit. But that is not actually the problem. People are getting excited and these circuits are just doing their own thing. The real problem is that there was just one Chabet, and not 500 others; *that*

would have been interesting and disruptive, but we could only do one. We need to figure out how to help create and equip a network that can produce 500 or 1,000 Chabets. That's where we need to be looking.

So again, in terms of equipping institutions, the Sri Lanka Archive of Art, Architecture, and Design is now raising money from major international foundations, and they are raising money locally. Now, whether they survive or not in the long run, how they grow, is in their hands. We wish them luck, watch their progress with interest, but their survival cannot be our struggle. We have to maintain our own trajectory and commitments. We have to work on our own survival plan.

AS

But it was through their initial contact with you that helped establish their credibility? You acted as a kind of incubator?

HN

They get credibility through association with our longer track record in the field of archives, and some umbrella money to get going. We wish for them to last forever. But even if they don't, hopefully they'll have a long enough lifespan to leave a lasting footprint. I don't think every project needs to survive forever; that's not the point. In any case, this model is what we're working with in Myanmar; we're bringing the Mobile Library there this year. We're trying not to let these projects become cookie cutters or templates. So, learning from our last project, before going there we had my colleague Susanna Chung, who heads our Learning & Participation activities, go to Yangon and meet with many people and organizations. We wanted a little map of what people there are interested in, what they're working on. Also, we're bringing the artist and teacher T. Shanathanan, who worked

exactly what animated the art historian Warburg throughout his life: "The whole problem of the legitimacy of emotional excess, or violent movement and gesture—*pathos*—in the visual art" became Warburg's concern.[34] He was obsessed with understanding how archaic experiences continued to be remembered, renewed, and gesturally expressed in European cultural productions. Thus, the object of his research was Memory; the primary material for this research were images, particularly reproductions. His technique for understanding these reproductions was association—or "Kombatibilität"[35] as he called it—and the practice was called "Ikonologie," the marrying of *eikon* (image) and *logos* (word).[36] In addition to owning a photographic collection of more than 25,000 images, according to a portrayal by Fritz Saxl, Warburg's friend, colleague, and librarian: "Books were for Warburg more than instruments of research. Assembled and grouped, they expressed the thought of mankind in its constant and in its changing aspects."[37] This notion resonates with Warburg's conviction that while images (art) can be read as scientific (historic) documents, they will always partly evade literal translation and impress us through direct, poetic force. In Warburg's practice, sense and meaning arise from *compatibility*—and thus precisely from the poetic connections made possible through the changing configuration and juxtaposition of singular material.

34 Morris Weitz, "*Aby Warburg: An Intellectual Biography* by E.H. Gombrich," *The Art Bulletin* 54, no. 1 (March 1972): 107.
35 See ibid., 109.
36 Warburg scholar Michael Diers states that "Das Wort zum Bild" was in fact one of Warburg's central mottos: see Diers, "Porträt aus Büchern: Stichworte zur Einfrührung," in *Porträt aus Büchern: Bibliothek Warburg und Warburg Institut Hamburg, 1933, London*, ed. Michael Diers (Hamburg: Dölling und Galitz Verlag, 1993), 18, with additional references.
37 Fritz Saxl, "The History of Warburg's Library," 328.

with us in Sri Lanka on the Jaffna leg of the Mobile Library, to use it as a vehicle for teaching art students; he'll come along to Yangon to share his experiences with university teachers and students, and also his use of the archival impulse in his own artistic practice.

E T

I find this relay structure for curating especially interesting, where the previous project sets up the working model for the next one, and the relay of potential transfers to new geographies and new concerns.

H N

Right, there is a Mumbai-based curatorial group called the Clark House Initiative, who have done an archival project on Burmese artists who were in exile in India and they are bringing out a book. We asked them what they were planning to do in Myanmar, but they were running out of funds as the book was printed. So by inviting them to take part in the program for Myanmar, we could also inject them into our conversation there. Because of this, the character of our library changes; it opens up to be partly about an Indian initiative looking at Burmese artists, and about Sri Lankan art students using the archive as fuel for their practice.

We are also working with the idea of digitization, especially as it is central to our partner, the Myanmar Art Resource Center and Archive (MARCA). But the digitization process is only part of the problem. There are always issues of context: Where will the digitized materials end up? How will the metadata be structured? How will we share these tools? We will invite one of our digital collections team members to run a digitization workshop. So again, we're looking to share tools as much as possible. One of the other strands of the project is about art ecologies, as a kind

of art history project. We are not doing complex, detailed analysis. Instead, we ask simple questions of the artists: Where did you learn? Who taught you? How did you make a living? Who wrote about your work? How did you exhibit it? How did your work travel? If you can get answers to these questions, what you have is the beginning of an art ecology, which is perhaps a different kind of art history than the detailed analysis of individual works—but a more interested and anchored account. This sort of thing lets us keep up with the kinds of practices that you are developing with *intercalations*: an expanded field of art and the curatorial, and the undisciplined discipline of these practices. Of course, that potential and that capacity was always there in art; it's just that our institutions and our lenses were such that we couldn't see it for what it was. It is important to say that we haven't invented this; it's just taken a while for the powers that stream through the art world to allow this sort of practice to be seen as legitimate and claim some space.

A S

I'd like to ask about the relationship between what the archive does and what the archive is—how the form affects the function, and vice versa. If the project of the AAA is understood as the co-production of certain constellations, or ecologies, or art practices, what is the broader strategy with respect to design?

H N

I think it also comes down to intent. Let me share with you an anecdote from a few years ago, when I was at Green Cardamom, about a publication called *Karkhana*. To make a long story short, we managed to reverse-engineer a major book project engaging the work of six (at that time) unknown Pakistani artists—each working in different cities

According to legend, at thirteen Aby Warburg, the eldest son of a family of German-Jewish bankers, ceded his birthright to his next younger brother, Max, in exchange for the promise that Max would forever after buy Aby all the books that he desired. Whether or not this story is true, Warburg indeed started to systematically collect books when he was twenty years old. While studying Renaissance painting in Florence and Strasbourg, he developed a strong desire for a type of library that would not impose the traditional boundaries of the disciplines, at that time often separated architectonically in different buildings and ideologically in different academic institutes.[38] In his effort to understand the influence of antiquity on subsequent Occidental culture, Warburg saw the division of genres as a fundamental obstacle. He felt that the knowledge of every relevant discipline needed to be mobilized together while being accessible in one space where the researcher could "wander from shelf to shelf."[39] By the time the Institute fled from the destruction of the Nazis, with their infamous book burnings and thought-policing and physical violence against citizens, to London in 1933, the Warburg Library consisted of 60,000 volumes. Originally, and with a smaller number of volumes, the collection had been kept in Warburg's private Hamburg home, but in 1926 a newly constructed library building was inaugurated just next door. Affiliated with the new University of Hamburg and open to professors and students, here the main reading room was designed as an oval "Denkraum" (a space of thought),

38 See ibid., 326: "But Warburg's plan was unusual; it did not fit into the official scheme which recognized only two categories, the small specialized library or the big universal storehouse of books."
39 Ibid.

around the world, but who all trained out of the same miniature painting program in Lahore—by staging a meaty but flashy US exhibition. It took two years to do it, but we ended up with a very costly publication. Part of the challenge of making that book involved figuring out how to talk about the work. Mirroring the six artists, we had six different approaches. One of us looked at the political economy of the artists' collaborations; another looked at the history of artist collaboration in Euro-America; another, the materials that were used in the work; Anna Sloan and I reflected on the economics and politics of the project; and so on. Anyway, the best way to describe the end result is a coffee table textbook. It had to be for the coffee table because it was the product of an exhibition, but that's not really it! This form was necessary to get the book produced, to make the work. There was an archival impulse driving the project. But that's only half of it; the other half was to track all the materials that went into the processes. It actually took about a year and half to get the artists to finally share all of the images they had used.

I'm telling you this story because one of the defining moments of my professional life in the art world came out of this. I got an email from UCLA asking permission to use one of the essays in the volume as part of their Art History Reader. So now, UCLA's art history students will be reading about this project and learn a bit of what it meant to grapple with archiving and collecting in collaboration with these Pakistani artists. This centrifugal effect of the book was very much a central part of our effort; we were trying to intervene in these major institutional texts. Again, it is the work of throwing grit into the smoothly functioning art machine. This is what we are trying to facilitate at the AAA. Not just by doing it ourselves, but also by equipping others to do so. I think there are many people who are working in this way and on many levels. One of those people, who had a formative impact on me, is Kobena Mercer. Do you know his four-volume *Annotating Art's Histories* project? It really opened things up for me. He's provided a range of tools for us all. So it is, in part, about confidence of form: there is a confidence of form in the printed book that I would argue is not yet matched by electronic forms of publishing, but this confidence is critical to meaning.

ET

I agree, but you would still admit that electronic publications have dramatically changed the archival impulse?

HN

Well, this is actually a very lively debate at the moment, even if the Archive only publishes a few books. *Mapping Asia*, published in May 2014, is an exception.[4] One of the reasons is that we have no distribution platform. So, part of the discussion about publishing printed matter is how to keep these books from being vanity projects. We thought we could use Art Basel in Hong Kong as a distribution mechanism, allowing us to reach at least some people we knew might be interested; but we can't reach everyone else who might also be interested if they came across it because we're not a big publisher. For the Archive, the choice between a printed matter release and digital dissemination isn't based on ideology; it's about strategy. While it is very easy for us to criticize academic journals, the process of double-blind peer review, and the cost of access to these publications, I don't think we can afford to be blind to the contact with other disciplines and the advantages of wider distribution that are made possible by linking with established, conventional publishing instruments. Part of the challenge is to

whose shape was probably an homage to Kepler's discovery of Mars's elliptical orbit.[40] The books were distributed across four floors following the basic thematic structure of "Orientation / Image / Word / Action."[41] In the 1920s, many public libraries were in the process of changing their cataloging and organizing principals to new systems that entailed storing the books out of sight so that users needed to request them from storage. In stark contrast, Warburg was convinced of something he called the "law of the good neighbor," which Saxl the librarian explains as follows: "The overriding idea was that the books together—each containing its larger or smaller bit of information and being supplemented by its neighbours—should by their titles guide the student to perceive the essential forces of the human mind and its history."[42] Intellectual research was therefore directly intertwined with, visually and spatially activated by, and made manifest in the library itself, which was correspondingly referred to more as a "Problembibliothek" (problem collection) rather than a "Büchersammlung" (book collection). Even though the importance of visual display, physical and temporary arrangement, and association was omnipresent throughout Warburg's research,[43] culminating in his

40 See Saxl, "Brief von Fritz Saxl an den Verlag B. G. Teubner, Leipzig," in *Aby Moritz Warburg: Der Bilderatlas Mnemosyne, Gesammelte Schriften*, Vol. 1, ed. Martin Warnke (Berlin: Akademie Verlag, 2000), xviii.

41 See Tilmann von Stockhausen, *Die Kulturwissenschaftliche Bibliothek Warburg: Architektur, Einrichtung und Organisation* (Hamburg: Verlag Dölling und Galitz, 1992), 75; and Saxl, "The History of Warburg's Library."

42 Ibid., 328.

43 According to the Warburg specialist Martin Warnke, Warburg's work was always articulated in part through exhibiting photographs and reproductions on panels displayed throughout the library. See Warnke, "Editorische Vorbemerkungen," in *Aby Moritz Warburg: Der Bilderatlas Mnemosyne, Gesammelte Schriften*, Vol. 1, ed. Martin Warnke, vii–iii.

corrupt neat disciplines by using their own instruments. We can inflect the content of these instruments. Maybe this isn't the stuff of revolution, but our contacts at many universities and art institutions might extend our collaborations into other projects, which can be very productive. That is our aim. Can we catalyze something? Can we enable something? But there is simply no way that we could produce all that we want to on our own. And the digital, of course, can be an optimistic space for collaboration.

AS

How does the archival impulse relate to your ambition for greater connectivity and affinity among various art practices? How would you characterize the role of the archive in lateral practices of contemporary knowledge production?

HN

That is a major question! Let me start again with an example. As part of our ongoing Bibliography of Modern and Contemporary Art Writing of India Project, we arranged several workshops last year. One of them took place at the Clark Art Institute in Massachusetts— the place that convenes the highest density of art historians in the world. Part of the idea was to look at tools and instruments for writing or challenging histories in South Asia. But a lot of the people doing art historical work on South Asia are getting their PhDs in the United States. Why wouldn't we engage these people? So, the Clark workshop was meant as a way to bring them into the conversation. Many of the participants had been Clark fellows. One of them pointed out that, in the Clark's collections, if you were looking for Van Gogh, you could find more than one and a half bookshelves worth of material. But when you look for material on Amrita Sher-Gil, for example, there are maybe two books and a little pamphlet.

So we wanted to ask about these discrepancies. But we also asked: why should this discrepancy preoccupy us? Because it is not a matter of volume, it is an issue of intensity. Maybe we really want the strong pills rather than the big buffets! This choice has implications for how we organize and structure events.

This question of choice brings us back to curating. There can be significant discomfort around curating. One of the internal discussions we've been having at the Archive is about the fact that we are always curating, selecting, and producing, so our mission should be to do this with as much transparency as we can muster. For us, there is no possibility of doing work that could approach anything like indexicality. So, if I were to rename AAA it could be *Asia? Art? Archive?* because in a way, that's how we function. We are still wrestling with the burden of what the name "archive" implies. To certain purists, we don't seem like an archive at all. Call us whatever you like, then, we are interested not simply in a definition of what we do, but what we can enable. To make things possible, we don't have to be part of a union with hidden codes or agendas; we have to be transparent, open about what we're doing, admit when our experiments fail, and be willing to drop things that are no longer relevant. Why should we go around taking photos at art openings and cataloging them on our website if this is already "archived" on Facebook? So, in part, we need to constantly be asking what we can stop doing, what is already curated elsewhere, so that we can focus on what we can be doing better and how we can better connect new nodes and new possibilities.

unfinished *Mnemosyne* panels, there was also a momentum at play regarding the books' performative role in knowledge creation. From a contemporary perspective, such a performance strikes a chord that is especially curatorial:

> The Warburg Library is both library and research institute. Its purpose is the examination of one problem and it advances this, first, by *displaying* the question that it pursues through the selection, collection, and arrangement of the books and pictorial material and, second, by *publishing* the outcomes of the research addressing the problem.[44]

Indeed, this approach produced very special effects:

> The arrangement of books was ... baffling and ... most peculiar, perhaps, was that Warburg never tired of shifting and re-shifting books. Every progress in his system of thought, every new idea about the interrelation of facts made him re-group the corresponding books. The library changed with every change in his research method and with every variation in his interests. Small as the collection was, it was intensely alive, and Warburg never ceased shaping it so that it might best express his ideas about the history of man.[45]

---

44   Saxl, "Die Kulturwissenschaftliche Bibliothek Warburg in Hamburg," in *Forschungs-institute: Ihre Geschichte, Organisation und Ziele*, Vol.2, ed. Ludolph Bauer, Albrecht Mendelssohn Bartholdy and Adolph Meyer (Hamburg: Paul Hartung, 1930), 355. With the aim of disseminating new research emerging from the environment of the library as well as establishing a tradition of Warburgian thought, two annual publication series were initiated after 1926, respectively called *Lectures* and *Studies*.
45   Saxl, "The History of Warburg's Library," 327.

1   Green Cardamom was a curatorial collective established in London, UK, in 2005, with the aim of presenting an Indian Ocean-centric view of the international art scene. In 2007, the collective opened an eponymously named London-based gallery; in 2012, in anticipation of his move to the Asia Art Archive, Hammad Nasar stepped down as Curatorial Director.

2   See the entry on the Asia Art Archive & Raking Leaves' *Open Edit: Mobile Library* project in Anna-Sophie Springer's "Reading Rooms Reading Machines" section of this book, 62.

3   Through #DataGrant and other adaptive, functional uses of the Twitter social media platform, the project PetaJakarta.org, co-directed by Etienne Turpin, attempts to restructure flood response and emergency management to better address the concerns and capacities of the urban poor in Jakarta. See info.petajakarta.org.

4   For more information on the *Mapping Asia* exhibition and publication, see http://aaa .org.hk/Programme/Details/540.

It is evident that in the round library of the Warburg Institute the books are not only conceived as content to be studied and built upon, but, like a curatorial arrangement, they are allowed to unfold aesthetically through their carefully arranged mutual proximity and adjacency. Assembled in a circular space that suggests the ongoing association of titles and the absence of hierarchy, of beginning and end, every idea ensues a display of new relations. As new "neighbors" are added, new constellations further engender new ideas. Philosophical, historical, and textual regimes are blurred with pictorial perspectives, allowing unstable meanings to emerge as the fruit of arrangement, context, *and* poetic force. In fact, the *Mnemosyne* panels in particular privilege visual relationships of proximity over textual explication, thus undermining a notion of knowledge "in straight lines" in favor of a field of knowledge that is constantly in motion.[46] Such a practice is less about the representation of fixed ideas than about dynamically provoking intellection through kaleidoscopic shifts. Even after the library was transformed into a publicly accessible institute, the holdings were organized in stark contrast to the horizontal principles of objectivity and rationalization introduced by Melvil Dewey; they were almost entirely customized according to Warburg's thesis regarding subjective needs and visual-cognitive perception. Yet, despite these radical gestures of affinity, the ordering principle of the library has reportedly posed challenges to users even if they were, or are, followers of the

---

46 For a book-length description of how Warburg can be said to have set the discipline of art history in motion, see Philippe-Alain Michaud, *Aby Warburg: The Image in Motion* (New York: Zone Books, 2004), including the foreword by Georges Didi-Huberman, "Knowledge: Movement (The Man Who Spoke to Butterflies)," 7–19.

     → Essay continues on page 99

Reading Rooms Reading Machines

A visual essay curated and annotated by Anna-Sophie Springer

> To admit authorities, however heavily furred and gowned, into our libraries and let them tell us how to read, what to read, what value to place upon what we read, is to destroy the spirit of freedom which is the breath of those sanctuaries. Everywhere else we may be bound by laws and conventions—there we have none.
>
> — Virginia Woolf, "How Should One Read a Book?", 1925

In a recent reflection on the conceptual impetus behind his publishing ventures in the early 1980s, Sanford Kwinter, the cofounder of *ZONE* and Zone Books, underscored a conceptual continuation between a book and the city as the guiding principle of his work on the border of editing and design. The publications were not, he writes, "to operate ... as a composition that referred to, or represented, the city beyond, but as a system of matter and force that would operate, whenever and however possible, in an unbroken continuity with, and as consubstantial to, the extended city itself."[1] The book and the city—environments in conjunction.

By configuring an associative sequence of artworks, idiosyncratic libraries, and unique bibliological apparatuses, the following visual essay—*Reading Rooms Reading Machines*—underscores the act of the book as both situation and practice, pushing it beyond the threshold of pagination into the prismatic realm of dimensionality and movement.

1   Sanford Kwinter, "Inside the Urban Azimuth (at the End of the Age of the Book)," *Harvard Design Magazine* 38, Summer 2014, www.harvarddesignmagazine.org/issues/38 /plumbing-the-urban-azimuth-at-the-end-of-the-age-of-the-book.

In the deserted room the silent
Book still journeys into time. And leaves
Behind it—dawns, night-watching hours,
My own life too, this quickening dream.

— from Jorge Luis Borges, "Ariosto and the Arabs"

The discourses referencing the Anthropocene inescap-
ably implicate concepts of time, existence, presence,
and disappearance by eliciting notions of deep time
that stretch backward into an unimaginably long-gone
past, as well as projecting into futures still tens of
thousands of years away. We ask: What is the planet
going to reveal of the human when humankind no
longer remains? And how should we act in the face of
finitude, not only of our own individual existence, but
of the species itself? Indeed, many scientists currently
argue that due to extreme weather events we are
facing an "apocalyptic" future well before the end of
this century.

With her latest project *Future Library* (2014–2114),
Scottish artist Katie Paterson embraces the book as a
true time machine able to help us fathom beyond our
own lifetime and sense of self, while affirming that
readers will persevere into the next century. Unfolding
over the coming 100 years, Paterson's highly conceptual Norway-based project consists of the estab-
lishment of a library whose texts will not become
available to its users until in 2114. Until then, a forest
of 1,000 newly planted trees is hoped to have grown
big enough to provide the material for the library's
paper and each year one commissioned author will
have contributed a new text to the growing archive of
100 pieces. While the literary works thus remain a gift
for future generations of readers yet-to-come, in 2018
a special room will be inaugurated in the Deichmanske
Public Library in Oslo where visitors can linger
and contemplate. Fittingly, the first author to create
a piece for the library is acclaimed Canadian writer
and environmental activist Margaret Atwood, known
for her speculative and often dystopian scenarios.
Images: Katie Paterson, *Future Library*, 2014–2114.
Top: Photograph © Bjørvika Utvikling by Kristin von
Hirsch. Bottom: © Katie Paterson. The project is
commissioned by Bjørvika Utvikling and produced
by Situations. Images courtesy of the artist.

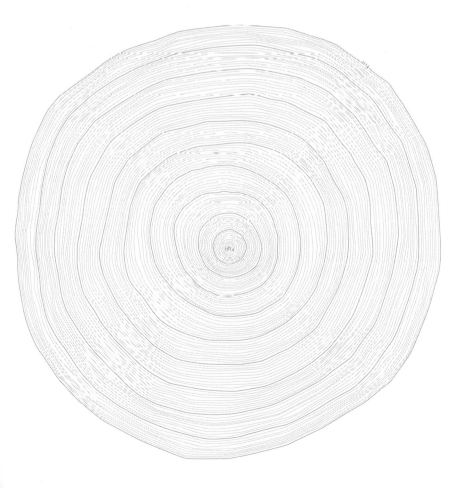

When the Gutenberg printing press was a new invention gradually turning the book into a real mass
medium, not everyone welcomed this technology
with enthusiasm and excitement. In a mode
of address similar to the contemporary skeptics
lamenting the death of the book in a world
of digitization, printed books on paper were also
once seen with suspicion by the monks occupied
in monastic scriptoria. Trained to copy texts on
parchment in meticulous handiwork, some of these
scribes doubted that the new books would even
last 100 years, as they believed these printed objects
to be less durable than the older tradition of the
manuscript (from Latin *manu*, "hand," and *scriptus*,
"written"). Image: A medieval scribe in his copying
chamber. Private collection.

The Reanimation Library is a growing book collection and publicly accessible reference library founded by NY-artist Andrew Beccone in 2006. Its repository consists of publications from the twentieth century whose textual information might now be outdated, but that remain fascinating visual sources thanks to their variegated picture contents. By resurrecting such a "fossil record" of illustrated books from used bookshops, yard and library sales, as well as dumps and the street, the Reanimation Library thus functions as a vast image archive of picture pages from all possible realms of printed knowledge. Scanners and photocopiers encourage users to freely incorporate the material into their own projects and thus to reassemble old content into new constellations. The library was originally located in Gowanus, Brooklyn, but recently moved to the Studio Wing of the Queens Museum, New York. Beccone also frequently follows invitations to set up temporary branches based on local book finds in other US locations, as well as in cities such as Mexico City and Beirut. Both an online catalog of titles and a collection of scanned images make the library available from anywhere, at www.reanimationlibrary.org. This photograph shows an installation view of the Reanimation Library, Highland Park Branch, Los Angeles, Monte Vista Projects. Image courtesy of Andrew Beccone. Photo by Aurora Tang.

↘ This medieval illustration from Guillaume de Tignonville, *Les dits moraux des philosophes*, Bourges, 1475, shows the controversial ancient Greek philosopher Diogenes surrounded by books in front of a peculiar reading room: his legendary barrel. Image courtesy of the Free Library of Philadelphia digital collection of medieval and Renaissance manuscripts.

What became known as The People's Library at Occupy Wall Street is an exceptional example of the important role books continue to play—despite the internet—whenever people are trying to change or challenge the systems that govern us. A cataloged system itself (with the first-ever recorded title paradigmatically being Hakim Bey's *T.A.Z.: The Temporary Autonomous Zone*), this community-driven and activist makeshift library, housed in tents and plastic boxes on the pavement of the Financial District, grew out of books that were dropped off at the site of the Wall Street protests since their beginning in September 2011. Its actual duration was rather short-lived; on November 15 of the same year, the NYPD seized and destroyed more than two-thirds of this

collection (originally almost 3,000 books) when they raided and vacated the premises of Zuccotti Park. Today this library no longer exists. As a result of a lawsuit filed by Occupy Wall Street against the City of New York (then still governed by Mayor Bloomberg), the material damages and loss of the book collection were met with a payment of $47,000 the following spring. The activist group distributed this compensation among other social groups, public institutions, and politically engaged businesses—many of them also working with and through books—such as Bluestockings Books, Books Through Bars, Free Press, and The New York Public Library. Photo by David Shankbone, 2011 (Creative Commons).

Mobile libraries and reading rooms have been a common phenomenon since at least the beginning of the twentieth century, forming a knowledge assemblage with donkeys, camels, ships, cars, and trains. This image depicts a visit of the Kentucky Guild Train and Kentucky Library Extension Bookmobile in 1961. The truck made books on arts and crafts available to visitors at the various stops along the route. Image courtesy the Electronic Records Archives of The Kentucky Department for Libraries and Archives.

Since 2011, the Asia Art Archive (AAA) in Hong Kong has organized the traveling project *Mobile Library* as a platform for cultural encounters. Each time it gathers and displays hundreds of different art publications—artists' books, catalogs, monographs, and magazines. After a first edition in Ho Chi Minh City, and more iterations in Jaffna and Colombo (Sri Lanka), the most recent exchange was developed in Myanmar. Collaborations with local galleries, publishers, universities, art and design schools encourage an active engagement with the material—resources that are often difficult to access in such a broad variety. Top and middle image: *Open Edit: Mobile Library*, Christa Seva Ashram, Chunnakam, Jaffna. Image courtesy Raking Leaves. Bottom image: *Open Talk*, Park Street Mews, Colombo, Sri Lanka. Image courtesy Raking Leaves. Photos by Sharni Jayawardena.

Since the Gutenberg printing press was invented in the fifteenth century, national libraries have continued to be significant icons of cultural identity and political independence. In 2002, editors from the Brooklyn-based *Cabinet Magazine* proclaimed their own territory, "Cabinetlandia," on a plot of land in the New Mexico desert. In 2004, through a collaboration with Matthew Passmore, a national library was erected there by half burying a metal filing cabinet into the earth, containing, among some other practical items, an index card catalog and magazine issues in plastic protection envelopes. Top image: Photo by Matthew Passmore. Copyright by Rebar Group, Inc., 2004. Bottom image: Matthew Passmore explores the "collection drawer" of the Cabinet National Library. Photo by John Bela. © Rebar Group, Inc. 2004. Both used with permission.

While many famed libraries have been lost throughout history, few have been given the chance to rebuild through the art of crowd-sourcing. During the war in Iraq, looters set fire to the library of the College of Fine Arts at the University of Baghdad, leading to the loss of over 70,000 books. In 2016, Wafaa Bilal created the installation *One Hundred Sixty-Eight Hours and One Second* at the Art Gallery of Windsor, Canada. The installation began with a library of blank white books as a monument to the loss of the library intended to activate the potential for rebuilding.

The project used the crowd-funding platform Kickstarter to raise funds for the purchase of new educational texts from a list compiled by faculty at the College of Fine Arts. *168:01* is thus a library of exchange, wherein each new text replaces a blank white book from the original installation. At the end of the exhibition, all of the books will be shipped to the College of Fine Arts in Baghdad to begin rebuilding the library. On 9 February 2016, the fundraising campaign ended; with the support of a platform-enabled community of donor-readers, the project was 654% funded. Wafaa Bilal, *168:01*, participatory installation, 2016. Copyright Wafaa Bilal. Courtesy Art Gallery of Windsor. Photo by Frank Piccolo.

Avant-garde Russian artist Aleksander Mikhailovich Rodchenko (1891–1956) was commissioned to design the *Workers' Club* as one element of the Soviet pavilion to the *Exposition internationale des arts décoratifs et industriels modernes* in Paris in the summer of 1925. The Club essentially reflected the revolutionary ideology of the new Soviet republic in which workers were to commune together in their leisure time, rather than withdraw into the solitary private space of the home as would have been customary in the old bourgeois system. Moreover, the notion of leisure itself was not one of relaxation and passivity, but focused on education and literacy. The centerpiece of the design was a table surrounded by twelve chairs, where the tabletop could be set to be flat for writing, or sloped for reading; a magazine rack provided the material to be studied. Harder to discern in this photograph is the chess table with two chairs, as well as the so-called Lenin Corner displaying photographs of the then recently deceased leader. Image: Aleksander Rodchenko, *Workers' Club*, Soviet Pavilion, *Exposition internationale des arts décoratifs et industriels modernes*, 1925. Image courtesy of Gallery Naruyama, Tokyo.

The Penguin Donkey Bookcase was designed by Egon Riss (1901–1964) and Jack Pritchard (1899–1992) in 1939, and manufactured by Isokon Furniture Ltd., London. Penguin press commissioned it specifically as a container for the new type of paperback book which, for the first time, made available high quality international literature to a wide public for the price of a pack of cigarettes (a distribution method copied by conceptual artists thirty years later with books such as Ed Ruscha's *Twentysix Gasoline Stations*, 1963, and Lawrence Weiner's *Statements*, 1968). The books were stacked in the side elements (appropriately referred to as panniers), while newspapers and magazines were slotted into the center. The Donkey's organic, curvilinear shape was achieved through the use of very thin plywood. The eruption of the Second World War thwarted the production of the Donkey. Approximately 100 were produced, and an original is now kept in the collection of the Victoria and Albert Museum, London. Image © Victoria and Albert Museum, London.

↖ In comparison to the modern natural history museum, the library is the older institution, and it served as a model for the organization and classification of natural history scholarship. Nowhere else is this relationship more directly articulated than in the xylotheque. Resembling shelved stacks of old tomes, in reality a xylotheque is a material encyclopedia of trees (indeed the base constituent of most papers). What appear like "books" are actually wooden containers holding replicas of the leaves and fruits of trees, while what seems like a thick leather binding reveals the texture of that tree's own bark. Often stunningly elaborate, xylotheques are a later form of botanical archive (following the earlier form of the herbarium). The earliest known example is the *Schildbachsche Holzbibliothek* (1771–99) at the Ottoneum, the natural history museum of Kassel. For dOCUMENTA (13), the artist Mark Dion designed a hexagonal oak wood display cabinet for its 530 different volumes. Image: Mark Dion, *Xylotheque* (2011–12). Wood, glass, electric lighting, porcelain cabinet knobs, wood inlay, plant parts, paper, papier-mâché, clay, wax, paint, wire, vellum, leather, plastic, ink. Installation view at dOCUMENTA (13). Image courtesy of the artist and Tanya Bonakdar Gallery, New York. Photos by Anders Sune Berg.

↘   "Elementarism" and an open and expansive sense of space characterized the approach of Austrian-American architect and designer Friedrich Kiesler (1890–1965), best known for his exhibition designs and his decades-long research on the cyclically shaped "Endless House." While the latter remained a multifaceted proposal, in the 1950s Kiesler was chief architect of the so-called "Shrine of the Book," a building which belongs to the Israel Museum in Jerusalem and houses ancient scriptures. Shortly after emigrating to the US, he became the founding director of the Laboratory of Design Correlation at Columbia University in 1937. The aim of the institute was to develop holistic—or better, correalistic—design products based on principles of "endlessness" as well as psychologies of perception. The flexibly designed *Mobile Home Library* was its first finalized product (developed in collaboration with students). It was published in the September 1939 issue of *Architectural Record*, "On Correalism and Biotechnique: Definition and Test of a New Approach to Building Design." Image © 2016 Austrian Frederick and Lillian Kiesler Private Foundation, Vienna. Photo © Ezra Stoller/Esto. All rights reserved.

In the mid 1970s, Donald Judd (1928–1994) moved from New York City to the small, West Texas town of Marfa. There he gradually purchased several former military, railroad, and bank buildings which he redesigned and used as spaces for making art and living among the vast steppes and open skies. One of the earliest building acquisitions was the so-called Block, a set of two WWI hangars, of which the eastern one in part was transformed into a personal library and reading room. Judd was a relentless reader and his collection comprises more than 13,000 titles. As if Marfa was to become his *Gesamtkunstwerk*, Judd designed the architectural modifications of all buildings and surrounding premises, the interior design, and a lot of the furniture himself. Thus the shelves, tables, and chairs in the library are of Judd's own iconic, minimalist design, and the books' organization, mainly by

themes, was determined by him as well. The shelves surrounding the table in the photograph, for example, cover "Old Europe," ranging from books on Ancient Greek, Etruscan, and Roman culture, to books on the Renaissance, Baroque, and also Viking mythology and classic British literature. A second room gathers volumes on and from the Americas, as well as those on flora and fauna, philosophy and political thought, and twentieth-century art and architecture. Today the premises are managed and preserved by the Judd Foundation; since his death, no item's position has been changed. Image of Donald Judd's private reading room at La Mansana de Chinati/The Block, South Library, Marfa, Texas.
© Judd Foundation Archive.

Situated inside a former reading room—which today comprises the main exhibition space of the Whitechapel Gallery—Kader Attia's expansive installation *Continuum of Repair: The Light of Jacob's Ladder* (2013) evokes both the library and the cabinet of curiosity as two seminal realms of historiography, cultural memory, and archival repository. Inside the room formed by an enormous structure of floor-to-ceiling bookshelves, each loaded with precious finds from various disciplines and epochs, one encounters a plywood vitrine displaying optical apparatuses such as telescopes and magnifying glasses, as well as scientific and spiritual lithographs dealing both with astronomy and the celestial imaginary. A collection of visual depictions of the biblical Jacob's Ladder is literally mirrored on the ceiling of the gallery where an infinitely reflected neon light soars the gaze upwards into a Borgesian shaft of books. Image: installation view at Whitechapel Gallery, London, 2013. Metal shelves, wooden vitrine, books, metallic stands, archival documents, lithographs, telescope, microscope, strip light, mirrors. Irene Panagopoulos Collection; courtesy of the artist; Galerie Nagel Draxler, Berlin/ Cologne; Galleria Continua, Les Moulins/Beijing; and, Galerie Krinzinger, Vienna. Image courtesy of the artist. Photo by Stephen White.

"It felt like being inside an enormous brain."
— Robert Musil on the library, 1930

No matter how advanced our technologies, humans remain the most essential of all Reading Rooms and Reading Machines; it is the boundless dimension of the literate minds, senses, and correlate imaginaries which surround the material repository of the library, the book, and the computer. Image on the left: A sectional view of the New York Public Library, Stephen A. Schwarzman Building, 42nd Street. Cover illustration, *Scientific American*, 27 May 1911. Image courtesy of the New York Public Library. Image on the right: Sectional view of the human brain, Plate 27 "Coupe de l'éncéphale sur le plan médian," Jean Marc Bourgery, *Traité complet de l'anatomie de l'homme comprenant la médicine operatoire par le docteur Bourgery, avec planche litographiées d'apres nature par N. H. Jacob*, Atlas, Vol. 3 (Paris: Delaunay, 1844). Image courtesy of the Universitätsbibliothek Heidelberg (Creative Commons).

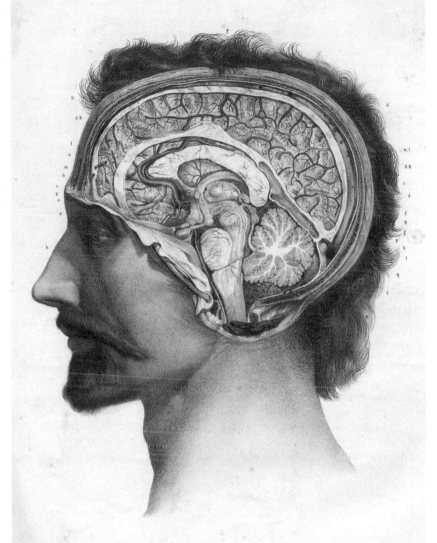

D'après nature par N.H. Jacob. Lith. par A. Leroux. Imp. Lemercier Benard et C.ie

André Malraux (1901–1976) was a French novelist, editor, and politician. In the 1920s, Malraux illustrated a number of books by experimenting with the page layout. As the art director at the acclaimed Paris publishing house Gallimard, through his own book series *Le Musée imaginaire* (1947–69), Malraux developed a visual rhetoric and theory of photographic reproduction and montage by joining and juxtaposing artworks otherwise far apart from each other—culturally, geographically, or historically—in a "museum without walls." Malraux thought that his utopian paper museum could be a unique and potentially comprehensive archive, able to present a retrospective of art unlike any traditional institution. In contrast to the common assumption that the photograph shown here documents Malraux working on the image order of his trilogy *Le Musée imaginaire de la sculpture mondial* from 1952–54, the scene is actually carefully staged. Produced for a story about Malraux in an issue of the French magazine *Paris Match* that appeared after the books were already published, the photo is rather a document of the highly conscious and strategic-artificial visual composer that Malraux was then; it is a record of the actual editorial work that went into the books themselves. Image: "Devant les photos illustrant son dernier livre, *Du Bas-relief aux grottes sacré es*, 2e tome du *Musée imaginaire*. Il en avait rassemblé 40.000 il en a choisi 190." From *Paris Match*, 19 June 1954, photograph by Maurice Jarnoux. Image: K. Verlag collection.

DEVANT LES PHOTOS IL

DERNIER LIVRE, « DU BAS-RELIEF AUX GROTTES SACRÉES », 2ᵉ TOME DU « MUSÉE IMAGINAIRE ». IL EN AVAIT RASSEMBLÉ 40.000. IL EN A CHOISI 390.

With his background in literary studies, Vancouver artist Rodney Graham has made several artworks dealing with books and their structure, as well as the activity of reading. In *Standard Edition* (1988), he transformed Sigmund Freud's *Complete Works* into a sculpture by embedding its twenty-four volumes in a "shelf" that evokes one of Donald Judd's minimalist wall objects. In contrast to this more formal intervention, in *Reading Machine for Lenz* (1993), Graham devised a structural means to intervene directly into a book's original literary narrative. As seen in the reproduction, this work consists of a revolving apparatus displaying

the first five pages of a particular edition of Georg Büchner's novella *Lenz*. The respective sentence breaks on pages 2 (top) and 5 (bottom) to create an endless narrative loop if juxtaposed directly, which is achieved through the rotational device. While Malraux used book spreads as a way to forge direct comparabilities between officially distant artworks, Graham mechanically unhinges an already existing page order so as to propose a new, originally unintended connection. Image courtesy of the MACBA Collection, MACBA Foundation, Barcelona. Photo by Tony Croll. © Rodney Graham.

An intense period of new discoveries and invention, the Renaissance also encouraged new modes of connection, arrangement, and display. Objects from art, science, and nature were presented in close proximity in cabinets of curiosities as the predecessors of the modern, disciplined museum. Moreover, new machines and engineering proposals were made available through printed collections of drawings and designs, commonly called "theaters of machines." Such assemblages of objects and pictures were also reflected in the realm of fiction. In Tomaso Campanella's literary utopia from 1602, *The City of the Sun*, the seven circular town walls are covered with encyclopedic, pictorial histories of all things and beings in the cosmos, as well as their internal orders and relations. Thus, the walls not only serve as protection from outside intruders, but also educate its citizens through a kind of ambient exposure from an early age. Another example of a circular device advancing knowledge and studious education through a sense of connectivity and display is Agostino Ramelli's engraving of an imaginary bookwheel, a wooden reading machine published in his book *Le diverse et artificiose machine* (1588). Ramelli envisioned that by sitting in front of this wheel—essentially a twelve-story lectern—and operating a rotational mechanism with one's feet, a reader would be able to easily alternate between different open volumes without having to move either oneself or the books—thus functioning not unlike a contemporary digital reading device. Even if originally unrealized, Ramelli's bookwheel has inspired many contemporary architects, artists, and scholars, such as Daniel Libeskind, who reconstructed it with his students on the occasion of the 1985 Venice Architecture Biennale, and historian of science Anthony Grafton, who has been using a similar device in his office at Princeton University for years. The most recent artistic rendering is Veronika Spierenburg's version entitled *Between Handle and Blade* (2013). Made of metal instead of wood at a diameter of three meters, the bookwheel was the main sculptural element of an artistic and curatorial project that Spierenburg realized from within the art library Kunstbibliothek Sitterwerk, St. Gallen to display—quite literally—rotating selections of books from the collections. Image courtesy of the artist. Photo by Katalin Deér, Sitterwerk, St. Gallen.

↖ The German art historian Aby Warburg (1866–1929) had started to collect books systematically when he was twenty years old. While studying Renaissance painting in Florence and Strasbourg, he had developed a strong desire for a type of library that would not impose the traditional boundaries of the disciplines, at that time often separated architectonically in different buildings and ideologically in different academic institutes. In 1926, a newly constructed library building was inaugurated next to Warburg's private home in Hamburg. The main reading room was designed as a circular *Denkraum* (a "space of thought"), and the books were distributed across four floors following the basic thematic structure of "Orientation / Image / Word / Action." Regarding his idiosyncratic book-ordering practice, Warburg was convinced of something he called the "law of the good neighbor," which the librarian Fritz Saxl has explained as follows: "The overriding idea was that the books together—each containing its larger or smaller bit of information and being supplemented by its neighbors—should by their titles guide the student to perceive the essential forces of the human mind and its history." It is Warburg's approach to the library as a "problem collection," a constellational, fluid space of shifting meanings and performances, rather than as a more-or-less static or preordained "object collection," that makes Warburg's personal library such an interesting model for curatorial and artistic practice. Image: Lesesaal, Kulturwissenschaftliche Bibliothek Warburg, Hamburg, Heilwigstraße 116, 1926. Courtesy of The Warburg Institute, London.

In Albrecht Dürer's engraving *Melencolia I* (1514), a winged figure sits amongst a series of human-made objects such as scales, compasses, an hourglass, a hammer, nails, and a ladder. But instead of using any of these measuring and construction devices, the angel seems deep in thought, staring ahead with a troubled frown, while in the background of the image the cosmos is opening up—half ocean, half sky, and in it a bright star, or maybe a radiating planet. This particular engraving was of the highest significance for Aby Warburg, whose research concerned the human passions and their iconological renderings across various epochs, and who created several *Mnemosyne* panels featuring this image. Composed many decades after the Warburg experiment, Lars von Trier's film *Melancholia* (2011) also conjures up this famous allegory on the relationship between the human and the cosmos. Like the angel in Dürer's picture, von Trier's heroine, Justine, is caught in a melancholic state of worldly disengagement. And, as in the engraving, a bright celestial body is looming in the sky, this time coming ever closer as an apocalyptic threat to the human world. As Warburg created thematic constellations of artworks on his black panels, von Trier's narrative unfolds, in part, from the affective reenactment of several iconic works from various artistic genres. Thus, for example, John Everett Millais's painting of *Ophelia* (1856) is evoked when Justine, the abandoned bride, is seen staring at the night sky while lying submerged in a creek. This painting appears once more in the very short scene where she maniacally re-curates a series of books openly displayed in her sister's library by exchanging the modernist art catalogs with catalogs containing figurative paintings. The images she selects create both a referential mirror for the many pictorial scenes quoted and restaged in the film, as well as an especially striking visual referent for Justine's own despair. Images: Film stills from Lars von Trier, *Melancholia*, 2011. Courtesy of Zentropa Entertainment, Hvidovre.

86d2. Dictionary Holder, with Casters. Price, $5.00.

86d3. With Side Shelf. Price, $6.50.

86d4. With Revolving Side Shelf. Price, $6.75.

86d5. With Central Revolving Shelf. Price, $6.75.

145

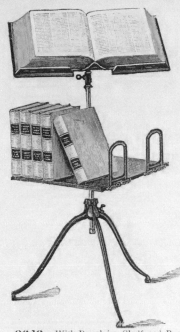

86d6. With Revolving Shelf and Book Supports. Price, $7.50.

86d7. With Revolving Bookcase. Price, $9.00.

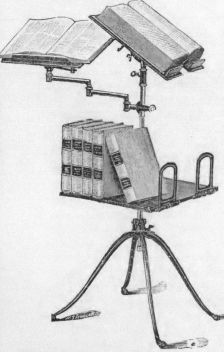

86d8. With Revolving Shelf and Book-Rest Attachment. Price, $9.50.

86d9. With 2 section Revolving Bookcase. Price, $13.00.

↖ Melvil Dewey (1851–1931) was the inventor of the Dewey Decimal Classification (DDC) system and an important figure in the development of modern library science and rationalistic library standards. He is less known for how he propagated these standards, not only through educational means such as founding the world's first school of librarianship at Columbia University in 1887, but also by establishing a company for library furniture and supplies in 1876. Aptly titled the Library Bureau, the firm advertised its product designs—and those of certified manufacturers such as Faber pencils from Germany or fireproof, cast-iron shelving systems made in the US—in sales catalogs for customers to order from. In the introduction to the *Illustrated Catalog* from 1890, the Library Bureau is described as supplying "everything needed" by public and private libraries and book owners, including several groundbreaking innovations: "The Card Index has a wider field today in business life than as the principal library catalog. The Shelf Sheet perforated blanks in binders are used instead of blank books, pamphlet cases for catalogs and price lists, scrapbooks for advertisements, notices and general notes." While these technologies today seem somewhat old-fashioned, the "L.B. Book Support Pat. 6 F. 1886" remains one of the most common bookstand designs to date (a metal plate cut once and bent into a ninety degree angle so that the weight of the books placed on the horizontal end ensures the vertical end to hold the books upright on the shelf). These pages display items seen much less frequently today: a series of reading stands with various shelving options. From *The Classified Illustrated Catalog of the Library Bureau Inc.: A Handbook of Library and Office Fittings and Supplies* (Boston: 1890), 144–45.

Many readers are now regularly exposed to reading rooms and reading machines that, in the 1890s, were still pure science fiction. As most of our reading today takes place online, mediated through the electronic screens of computers, smartphones, e-readers, etc., the internet might well be the biggest reading room ever—and thus maybe the closest realization of a Borgesian Library containing all text and hypertext, all knowledge and hyper-knowledge. Several large projects are currently processing entire libraries in order to transform actual books into digital records and thereby make their contents remotely accessible. The most extensive experiment in digitization is Google's Library Project, initiated in 2004 in collaboration with major university libraries; but there are also others, such as the Internet Archive, HathiTrust, and Project Gutenberg (all of which in part still draw on resources scanned by Google). The online community Arg.org remains exceptional among these services in that it is nearly entirely dependent on the participation of the community of its users to both upload PDFs and e-book files, and to organize this material by filling out "index cards" and creating thematic "stacks." This active participation in developing and maintaining the Arg.org library stands in stark contrast to Google's efforts of producing the impression of a seamless and fully automatized digitization process. Resonant with Arg.org's spirit of do-it-yourself scanning, this image belongs to an open-source tutorial on how to cheaply build one's own Linear Book Scanner, a device that prevents book spine damage and which was originally developed for no other client than Google itself. Image courtesy of Dany Qumsiyeh from http://linearbookscanner.org.

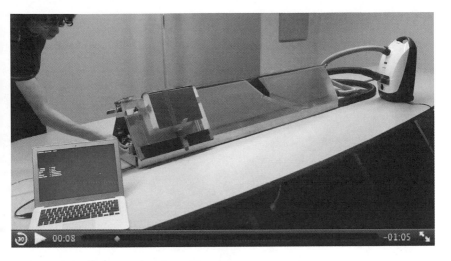

A book moves back and forth over the machine.

Each time across, a vacuum sucks a page from one side to the other.

The pages are scanned as they travel across two imaging sensors.

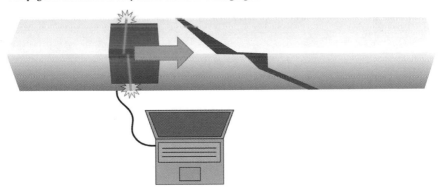

Gustave Flaubert (1821–1880) reported that his encounter with Pieter Brueghel the Younger's Renaissance painting *The Temptation of Saint Anthony* (c. 1608) in Italy was the inspiration for working on his epic book of the same title, *La Tentation de saint Antoine* (1874). The connection he felt to the story and its depiction was so strong that, in order to contemplate it without interruption, Flaubert bought his own copy of the work—the etching by Brueghel's disciple Jacques Callot, shown here, from 1635. Image courtesy of the National Gallery of Canada, Ottawa.

RILIERE COMITI CONSISTORIANO SACRARVM IVSSIONVM VIRO
T CONSECRATQVE.

Sancte senex, tantos tantos et despicis hostes?
Hic spirat mortale nibi, nec Gaudia pectus.
Blanda mouent, nec frangit Amor, nec funera terrat.
Bellus infixa polo reparans que ab Origine traxu
Sustinet in terris quas videt in æthere pugnas

Letter to the Superior Court of Quebec Regarding Arg.org

Charles Stankievech
19 January 2016

To the Superior Court of Quebec:

I am writing in support of the online community and library platform called "Arg.org" (also known under additional aliases and
urls including "aaaaarg.org," "grr.aaaaarg.org," and most recently
"grr.aaaaarg.fail"). It is my understanding that a copyright infringement lawsuit has been leveled against two individuals who
support this community logistically. This letter will address what
I believe to be the value of Arg.org to a variety of communities
and individuals; it is written to encompass my perspective on the
issue from three distinct positions: (1) As Director of the Visual
Studies Program, Faculty of Architecture, Landscape, and Design,
University of Toronto, where I am a professor and oversee three
degree streams for both graduate and undergraduate students;
(2) As the co-director of an independent publishing house based
in Berlin, Germany, and Toronto, Canada, which works with international institutions around the world; (3) As a scholar and writer
who has published in a variety of well-regarded international
journals and presses. While I outline my perspective in relation to
these professional positions below, please note that I would also
be willing to testify via video-conference to further articulate
my assessment of Arg.org's contribution to a diverse international
community of artists, scholars, and independent researchers.

"Warburgian tradition."[47] If we consider the Warburg Library in its simultaneous role as a contained space and the reflection of an idiosyncratic mental energy, General Stumm's aforementioned feeling of "entering an enormous brain" seems an especially concise description. Indeed, for Saxl the librarian, "the books remain a body of living thought as Warburg had planned,"[48] showing "the limits and contents of his scholarly worlds."[49] Developed as a research tool to solve a particular intellectual problem—and comparable on a number of levels to exhibition-led inquiry—Aby Warburg's organically structured, themed library is a three-dimensional instance of a library that performatively articulates and potentiates itself, which is not yet to say *exhibits*, as both spatial occupation and conceptual arrangement, where the order of things emerges experimentally, and in changing versions, from the collection and its unusual cataloging.[50]

47 Saxl speaks of "many tentative and personal excrescences" ("The History of Warburg's Library," 331). When Warburg fell ill in 1920 with a subsequent four-year absence, the library was continued by Saxl and Gertrud Bing, the new and later closest assistant. Despite the many helpers, according to Saxl, Warburg always remained the boss: "everything had the character of a private book collection, where the master of the house had to see it in person that the bills were paid in time, that the bookbinder chose the right material, or that neither he nor the carpenter delivering a new shelf over-charged" (Ibid., 329).

48 Ibid., 331.

49 Ibid., 329.

50 A noteworthy aside: Gertrud Bing was in charge of keeping a meticulous index of names and keywords; evoking the library catalog of Borges's fiction, Warburg even kept an "index of un-indexed books." See Diers, "Porträt aus Büchern," 21.

1. Arg.org supports a collective & semiprivate community of academics & intellectuals.

As the director of a graduate-level research program at the University of Toronto, I have witnessed first-hand the evolution of academic research. Arg.org has fostered a vibrant community of thinkers, students, and writers, who can share their research and create new opportunities for collaboration and learning because of the knowledge infrastructure provided by the platform. The accusation of copyright infringement leveled against the community misses the point of the research platform altogether. While there are texts made available for download at no expense through the Arg.org website, it is essential to note that these texts are not advertised, nor are they accessible to the general public. Arg.org is a private community whose sharing platform can only be accessed by invitation. Such modes of sharing have always existed in academic communities; for example, when a group of professors would share Xerox copies of articles they want to read together as part of a collaborative research project. Likewise, it would be hard to imagine a community of readers at any time in history without the frequent lending and sharing of books. From this perspective, Arg.org should be understood within a twenty-first century digital ethos, where the sharing of intellectual property and the generation of derivative IP occurs through collaborative platforms. On this point, I want to draw further attention to two fundamental aspects of Arg.org.

a. One essential feature of the Arg.org platform is that it gives invited users the ability to create reading lists from available texts—what are called on the website "collections." These collections are made up of curated folders containing text files (usually in Portable Document Format); such collections allow for new and novel associations of texts, and the development of working bibliographies that assist in research. Users can discover previously unfamiliar materials—including entire books and excerpted chapters, essays, and articles—through these shared collections. Based on the popularity of previous collections I have personally assembled on the Arg.org platform, I have been invited to give

In the Memory Hall of Reproductions

Several photographs document how the Warburg Library was also a backdrop for Warburg's picture panels, the wood boards lined with black fabric, which, not unlike contemporary mood boards, held the visual compositions he would assemble and re-assemble from around 2,000 photographs, postcards, and printed reproductions cut out of books and newspapers. Sometimes accompanied by written labels or short descriptions, the panels served as both public displays and research-in-process, and were themselves photographed with the aim to eventually be disseminated as book pages in publications. In the end, not every publishing venture was realized, and most panels themselves were even lost along the way; in fact, today, the panel photographs are the only visual remainder of this type of research from the Warburg Institute. Probably the most acclaimed of the panels are those which Warburg developed in close collaboration with his staff during the last years of his life and from which he intended to create a sequential picture atlas of human memory referred to as the *Mnemosyne Atlas*. Again defying the classical boundaries of the disciplines, Warburg had appropriated visual material from the archives of art history, natural philosophy, and science to vividly evoke and articulate his thesis through the creation of unprecedented associations. Drawing an interesting analogy, the following statement from Warburg scholar Kurt Forster underlines the importance of the panels for the creation of meaning:

> Warburg's panels belong into the realm of the mon-
> tage à la Schwitters or Lissitzky. Evidently, such a

guest lectures at various international venues; such invitations demonstrate that this cognitive work is considered original research and a valuable intellectual exercise worthy of further discussion.

b. The texts uploaded to the Arg.org platform are typically documents scanned from the personal libraries of users who have already purchased the material. As a result, many of the documents are combinations of the original published text and annotations or notes from the reader. Commentary is a practice that has been occurring for centuries; in Medieval times, the technique of adding commentary directly onto a published page for future readers to read alongside the original writing was called "Glossing." Much of the philosophy, theology, and even scientific theories were originally produced in the margins of other texts. For example, in her translation and publication of Charles Babbage's lecture on the theory of the first computer, Ada Lovelace had more notes than the original lecture. Even though the text was subsequently published as Babbage's work, today modern scholarship acknowledges Lovelace as important voice in the theorization of the modern computer due to these vital marginal notes.

2. Arg.org supports small presses.
Since 2011, I have been the co-founder and co-director of K. Verlag, an independent press based in Berlin, Germany, and Toronto, Canada. The press publishes academic books on art and culture, as well as specialty books on art exhibitions. While I am aware of the difficulties faced by small presses in terms of profitability, especially given fears that the sharing of books online could further hurt book sales; however, my experience has been in the opposite direction. At K. Verlag, we actually upload our new publications directly to Arg.org because we know the platform reaches an important community of readers and thinkers. Fully conscious of the uniqueness of printed books and their importance, digital circulation of ebooks and scanned physical books present a range of different possibilities in reaching our audiences in a variety of ways. Some members of Arg.org may be too

comparison does not need to claim artistic qualities for Warburg's panels, nor does it deny them regarding Schwitters's or Lissitzky's collages. It simply lifts the role of graphic montage from the realm of the formal into the realm of the construction of meaning.[51]

Interestingly, even if Forster makes a point not to categorize Warburg's practice as art, in twentieth-century art theory and visual culture scholarship, his idiosyncratic technique has evidently been mostly associated with art practice. In fact, insofar as Warburg is acknowledged (together with Marcel Duchamp and, perhaps, the less well-known André Malraux), it is as one of the most important predecessors for artists working with the archive.[52] Forster articulates the traditional assumption that only artists were "allowed" to establish idiosyncratic approaches and think with objects outside of the box. However, within the relatively new discourse of the "curatorial," contra the role of the "curator," the curatorial delineates its territory as that which is no longer defined exclusively by what the curator *does* (i.e. responsibilities of classification and care) but rather as a particular agency in terms of epistemologically and spatially working with existing materials and collections. Consequently, figures such as Warburg

51   Kurt Forster, quoted in Benjamin H.D. Buchloh, "Gerhard Richter's Atlas: Das anomische Archiv," in *Paradigma Fotografie. Fotokritik am Ende des fotografischen Zeitalters*, ed. Herta Wolf (Frankfurt/M.: Suhrkamp Verlag, 2002), 407, with further references.

52   One such example is the *Atlas* begun by Gerhard Richter in 1962; another is Thomas Hirschhorn's large-format, mixed-media collage series *MAPS*. Entitled *Foucault-Map* (2008), *The Map of Friendship Between Art and Philosophy* (2007), and *Hannah-Arendt-Map* (2003), these works are partly made in collaboration with the philosopher Marcus Steinweg. They bring a diverse array of archival and personal documents or small objects into associative proximities and reflect the complex impact philosophy has had on Hirschhorn's art and thinking.

poor to afford to buy our books (eg. students with increasing debt, precarious artists, or scholars in countries lacking accessible infrastructures for high-level academic research). We also realize that Arg.org is a library-community built over years; the site connects us to communities and individuals making original work and we are excited if our books are shared by the writers, readers, and artists who actively support the platform. Meanwhile, we have also seen that readers frequently discover books from our press through a collection of books on Arg.org, download the book for free to browse it, and nevertheless go on to order a print copy from our shop. Even when this is not the case, we believe in the environmental benefit of Arg.org; printing a book uses valuable resources and then requires additional shipping around the world—these practices contradict our desire for the broadest dissemination of knowledge through the most environmentally-conscious of means.

3. Arg.org supports both official institutional academics
& independent researchers.
As a professor at the University of Toronto, I have access to one of the best library infrastructures in the world. In addition to core services, this includes a large number of specialty libraries, archives, and massive online resources for research. Such an investment by the administration of the university is essential to support the advanced research conducted in the numerous graduate programs and by research chairs. However, there are at least four ways in which the official, sanctioned access to these library resources can at times fall short.

a. Physical limitations. While the library might have several copies of a single book to accommodate demand, it is often the case that these copies are simultaneously checked out and therefore not available when needed for teaching or writing. Furthermore, the contemporary academic is required to constantly travel for conferences, lectures, and other research obligations, but travel-ling with a library is not possible. Frequently while I am working abroad, I access Arg.org to find a book which I have previously and Malraux, who thought apropos objects in space (even when those objects are dematerialized as reproductions), become productive forerunners across a range of fields: from art, through cultural studies and art history, to the curatorial.

Essential to Warburg's library and *Mnemosyne Atlas*, but not yet articulated explicitly, is that the practice of constructing two-dimensional, heterogeneous image clusters shifts the value between an original work of art and its mechanical reproduction, anticipating Walter Benjamin's essay written a decade later.[53] While a museum would normally exhibit an original of Albrecht Dürer's *Melencolia I* (1514) so it could be contemplated aesthetically (admitting that even as an etching it is ultimately a form of reproduction), when inserted as a quotidian reprint into a Warburgian constellation and exhibited within a library, its "auratic singularity"[54] is purposefully challenged. Favored instead is the iconography of the image, which is highlighted by way of its embeddedness within a larger (visual-emotional-intellectual) economy of human consciousness.[55] As it receives its impetus from the interstices

53   One of the points Benjamin makes in "The Artwork in the Age of Mechanical Reproduction" is that reproducibility increases the "exhibition value" of a work of art, meaning its relationship to being viewed is suddenly valued higher than its relationship to tradition and ritual ("cult value"); a process which, as Benjamin writes, nevertheless engenders a new "cult" of remembrance and melancholy (224–26).

54   Benjamin defines "aura" as the "here and now" of an object, that is, as its spatial, temporal, and physical presence, and above all, its uniqueness—which in his opinion is lost through reproduction. Ibid., 222.

55   It is worth noting that Warburg wrote his professorial dissertation on Albrecht Dürer. Another central field of his study was astrology, which Warburg examined from historical and philosophical perspectives. It is thus not surprising to find out that Dürer's *Melencolia I* (1514), addressing the relationship between the human and the cosmos, was of the highest significance to Warburg as a recurring theme. The etching is shown, for instance, as image 8 of Plate 58, "Kosmologie bei Dürer" (Cosmology in Dürer); reproduced in Warnke, ed., *Aby Moritz Warburg: Der Bilderatlas Mnemosyne, Gesammelte Schriften*, Vol. 1, 106–7. The connections

purchased, and which is on my bookshelf at home, but which is not in my suitcase. Thus, the Arg.org platform acts as a patch for times when access to physical books is limited—although these books have been purchased (either by the library or the reader herself) and the publisher is not being cheated of profit.

b. Lack of institutional affiliation. The course of one's academic career is rarely smooth and is increasingly precarious in today's shift to a greater base of contract sessional instructors. When I have been in-between institutions, I lost access to the library resources upon which my research and scholarship depended. So, although academic publishing functions in accord with library acquisitions, there are countless intellectuals—some of whom are temporary hires or in-between job appointments, others whom are looking for work, and thus do not have access to libraries. In this position, I would resort to asking colleagues and friends to share their access or help me by downloading articles through their respective institutional portals. Arg.org helps to relieve this precarity through a shared library which allows scholarship to continue; Arg.org is thus best described as a community of readers who share their research and legally-acquired resources so that when someone is researching a specific topic, the adequate book/essay can be found to fulfill the academic argument.

c. Special circumstances of non-traditional education. Several years ago, I co-founded the Yukon School of Visual Arts in Dawson City as a joint venture between an Indigenous government and the State college. Because we were a tiny school, we did not fit into the typical academic brackets regarding student population, nor could we access the sliding scale economics of academic publishers. As a result, even the tiniest package for a "small" academic institution would be thousands of times larger than our population and budget. As a result, neither myself nor my students could access the essential academic resources required for a post-secondary education. I attempted to solve this problem by forging partnerships, pulling in favors, and accessing resources through platforms like Arg.org. It is important to realize

among text and image, visual display and publishing, the expansive space of the library and the dense volume of the book, Aby Warburg's wide-ranging work appears to be best summarized by the title of one of the *Mnemosyne* plates: "Book Browsing as a Reading of the Universe."[56]

To the Paper Museum

Warburg had already died before Benjamin theorized the impact of mechanical reproduction on art in 1935. But it is Malraux who claims to have embarked on a lengthy, multi-part project about similitudes in the artistic heritage of the world in exactly the same year, and for whom, in opposition to the architectonic space of the museum, photographic reproduction, montage, and the book are the decisive filters through which one sees the world. At the outset of his book *Le Musée imaginaire* (first published in 1947),[57] Malraux argues that the secular modern museum has been crucial in reframing and transforming objects into art, both by displacing them from their original sacred or ritual context and purpose, and by bringing them into proximity and adjacency with one another, thereby opening new possible readings

and analogies between Warburg's image-based research and his theoretical ideas, and von Trier's *Melancholia*, are striking; see Anna-Sophie Springer's visual essay "Reading Rooms Reading Machines" on p. 91 of this book.

56   "Buchblättern als Lesen des Universums," Plate 23a, reproduced in Warnke, *Aby Moritz Warburg: Der Bilderatlas Mnemosyne, Gesammelte Schriften*, Vol. 1, 38–9.

57   The title of the English translation, *The Museum Without Walls*, by Stuart Gilbert and Francis Price (London: Secker & Warburg, 1967), must be read in reference to Erasmus's envisioning of a "library without walls," made possible through the invention of the printing press, as Anthony Grafton mentions in his lecture, "The Crisis of Reading," The CUNY Graduate Center, New York, 10 November 2014.

that Arg.org was founded to meet these grassroots needs; the platform supports a vast number of educational efforts, including co-research projects, self-organized reading groups, and numerous other non-traditional workshops and initiatives.

d. My own writing on Arg.org. While using the platform, I have frequently come across my own essays and publications on the site; although I often upload copies of my work to Arg.org myself, these copies had been uploaded by other users. I was delighted to see that other users found my publications to be of value and were sharing my work through their curated "collections." In some cases, I held outright exclusive copyright on the text and I was pleased it was being distributed. In other rare cases, I shared the copyright or was forced to surrender my IP prior to publication; I was still happy to see this type of document uploaded. I realize it is not within my authority to grant copyright that is shared, however, the power structure of contemporary publishing is often abusive towards the writer. Massive, for-profit corporations have dominated the publishing of academic texts and, as a result of their power, have bullied young academics into signing away their IP in exchange for publication. Even the librarians at Harvard University—who spend over $3.75 million USD annually on journal subscriptions alone—believe that the economy of academic publishing and bullying by a few giants has crossed a line, to the point where they are boycotting certain publishers and encouraging faculty to publish instead in open access journals.

I want to conclude my letter of support by affirming that Arg.org is at the cutting edge of academic research and knowledge production. Sean Dockray, one of the developers of Arg.org, is internationally recognized as a leading thinker regarding the changing nature of research through digital platforms; he is regularly invited to academic conferences to discuss how the community on the Arg.org platform is experimenting with digital research. Reading, publishing, researching, and writing are all changing rapidly as networked digital culture influences professional and academic life more and more frequently. Yet, our legal frameworks and business models are always slower than the practices ("metamorphoses") of individual objects—and, even more critically, producing the general category of art itself. As exceptions to this process, Malraux names those creations that are so embedded in their original architecture that they defy relocation in the museum (such as church windows, frescoes, or monuments); this restriction of scale and transportation, in fact, resulted in a consistent privileging of painting and sculpture within the museological apparatus.[58]

Long before networked societies, with instant Google Image searches and prolific photo blogs, Malraux dedicated himself to the difficulty of accessing works and oeuvres distributed throughout an international topography of institutions. He located a revolutionary solution in the dematerialization and multiplication of visual art through photography and print, and, above all, proclaimed that an *imaginary museum* based on reproductions would enable the completion of a meaningful collection of artworks initiated by the traditional museum.[59] Echoing Benjamin's theory regarding the power of the reproduction to change how art is perceived, Malraux writes, "Reproduction is not the origin but a decisive means for the process of intellectualization to which we subject art.

58   I thank the visual culture scholar Antonia von Schöning for pointing me to Malraux after reading my previous considerations of the book-as-exhibition. Von Schöning herself is author of the essay "Die universelle Verwandtschaft zwischen den Bildern: André Malraux' *Musée Imaginaire* als Familienalbum der Kunst," *kunsttexte.de*, April 2012, edoc.hu-berlin.de/kunsttexte/2012-1/von-schoening -antonia-5/PDF/von-schoening.pdf.

59   André Malraux, *Psychologie der Kunst: Das imaginäre Museum* (Baden-Baden: Woldemar Klein Verlag, 1949), 9; see also Rosalind Krauss, "The Ministry of Fate," in *A New History of French Literature*, ed. Denis Hollier (Cambridge, MA and London: Harvard University Press, 1989), 1000–6: "The photographic archive itself, insofar as it is the locale of a potentially complete assemblage of world artifacts, is a repository of knowledge in a way that no individual museum could ever be" (1001).

of artists and technologists. Arg.org is a non-profit intellectual venture and should therefore be considered as an artistic experiment, a pedagogical project, and an online community of co-researchers; it should not be subject to the same legal judgments designed to thwart greedy profiteers and abusive practices. There are certainly some documents to be found on Arg.org that have been obtained by questionable or illegal means—every Web 2.0 platform is bound to find such examples, from Youtube to Facebook; however, such examples occur as a result of a small number of participant users, not because of two dedicated individuals who logistically support the platform. A strength of Arg.org and a source of its experimental vibrancy is its lack of policing, which fosters a sense of freedom and anonymity which are both vital elements for research within a democratic society and the foundations of any library system. As a result of this freedom, there are sometimes violations of copyright. However, since Arg.org is a committed, non-profit community-library, such transgressions occur within a spirit of sharing and fair use that characterize this intellectual community. This sharing is quite different from the popular platform Academia.edu, which is searchable by non-users and acquires value by monetizing its articles through the sale of digital advertising space and a nontransparent investment exit strategy. Arg.org is the antithesis of such a model and instead fosters a community of learning through its platform.

Please do not hesitate to contact me for further information, or to testify as a witness.

Regards,
Charles Stankievech,
Director of Visual Studies Program, University of Toronto
Co-Director of K. Verlag, Berlin & Toronto

… Medieval works, as diverse as the tapestry, the glass window, the miniature, the fresco, and the sculpture become united as one family if reproduced together on one page."[60] In his search for a common visual rhetoric, Malraux went further than merely arranging creations from one epoch and cultural sphere by attempting to collect and directly juxtapose artworks and artifacts from very diverse and distant cultural, historical, and geographic contexts.

His richly illustrated series of books thus functions as a utopian archive of new temporalities of art liberated from history and scale by de-contextualizing and re-situating the works, or rather their reproduced images, in unorthodox combinations. *Le Musée imaginaire* was thus an experimental virtual museum intended to both form a repository of knowledge and provide a space of association and connection that could not be sustained by any other existing place or institution. From an art historical point of view—Malraux was not a trained scholar and was readily criticized by academics—his theoretical assumptions of "universal kinship" (von Schöning) and the "anti-destiny" of art have been rejected. His material selection process and visual appropriation and manipulation through framing, lighting, and scale, have also been criticized for their problematic and often controversial—one could say, colonizing—implications.[61] Among the most recent critics is the art historian Walter Grasskamp, who argues that Malraux moreover might well have plagiarized the image-based work of the

60   André Malraux, *Das imaginäre Museum*, 16.
61   See the two volumes of Georges Duthuit, *Le Musée Inimaginable* (Paris: J. Corti, 1956); Ernst Gombrich, "André Malraux and the Crisis of Expressionism," *The Burlington Magazine* 96 (1954): 374–78; Michel Merlot, "L'art selon André Malraux, du Musée imaginaire à l'Inventaire general," *In Situ* 1 (2001), www.insitu.revues .org/1053; and von Schöning, "Die universelle Verwandtschaft zwischen den Bildern."

Andrew Norman Wilson, *Museum Metallicum Autoris – 35*, 2012. Courtesy of the artist.

French photographer André Vigneau, who had published juxtapositions of art historical photographs in his series of *fascicules*, entitled *Encyclopédie photographique de l'art*, as early as 1935 and whose photographs in part reappeared in Malraux's own compositions.[62] Nevertheless, Malraux's progressive experiment of replacing the traditional museum with constellations of images arranged on the pages of a printed photo book opens up an alternative genealogy for curatorial practices focusing on the library. What Malraux's work foregrounds most profoundly is the potential of a paper museum based entirely on reproductions. But it is also important to note that Malraux's strategy functions through the psychological mechanism of melancholy embedded in the ideology of the library: the tension between cloistered seclusion and cosmopolitan exposure is, for the library, a melancholic celebration of finding both refuge from the world and the site of ritual. In 1973, the Fondation Maeght in Saint-Paul-de-Vence near Nice presented the exhibition *Le Musée imaginaire d'André Malraux*, which, despite its ambition, was seen by Malraux as a disappointment. Summoning Harald Szeemann's much later utopia, "The Museum of Obsessions," Malraux's imaginary museum is less suited for the space of the gallery, and inclined instead toward the library, with its book stacks, silent reading voices, and vivid mental worlds; indeed, *Les Voix du silence* is the title of the second part of his trilogy published in 1951. The reason for the gallery exhibition's failure can be attributed to a confusion between the space of the museum and the space of the library:

62   Walter Grasskamp, *André Malraux und das imaginäre Museum: Die Weltkunst im Salon* (München: C.H. Beck, 2014), 61–74. Here, Grasskamp also emphasizes the marginalized role of contributing image archives and practicing photographers questioning Malraux's role as autonomous author and ingenious creator.

The Ethics of the Book (Beyond Species Nostalgia)

Joanna Zylinska (JZ) in conversation
with Anna-Sophie Springer (AS)
& Etienne Turpin (ET)

Our *Fantasies of the Library* would remain incomplete without an attendant reconsideration of the book as printed matter in the age of the Anthropocene. As readers are increasingly drawn to digital sources for access to materials and to digital platforms as reading devices, the efficacy of the book seems more unstable than ever. Despite these trends, philosophers and media theorists insist on the fundamental instability of the book, not merely as a result of the digital turn, but as an essential dimension of the codex understood as a technology of thought. In this interview, conducted in London in October 2014 following the book launch of Joanna Zylinska's *Minimal Ethics for the Anthropocene* at Goldsmiths, University of London, editors Anna-Sophie Springer and Etienne Turpin discuss the contours of the book as a series of platforms, enterprises, and collaborations with Joanna. The following edited version of this conversation is an attempt to delineate an ethics of the book as a decisively human technology of thought, beyond any species nostalgia, be it humanist or posthuman.[1]

ET

I'd like to begin with the question of how you approach the book in the *Living Books About Life* project. As I understand it, you invite humanities scholars to curate living publications of scientific content. Why?

JZ

Living Books About Life is a project run by myself and media theorists Gary Hall and Claire Birchall, in association with Open Humanities Press. What we were originally trying to achieve with the curation of science content was to go beyond the public-understanding-of-science agenda—the one that says "let's just make science palatable to humanities scholars and to the lay public." We also took inspiration from the sciences themselves. Indeed, scientists have been much more radical in their adoption of open access, as you well know, than humanities scholars …

ET

Some of the highest ranked journals in biology and the biological sciences are open access.

JZ

Yes, similarly arXiv.org is a very important online repository for physics scholarship. One of the reasons scientists

the former is based on a series of sacramental characteristics, while the latter is premised on the melancholic. For, following Benjamin, the original work of art and the reproduction differ in terms of "cult value" versus "exhibition value"; while the former is charged with an aura of rarity and authority, the latter is characterized by ideas of both loss and replacement—a dynamic, in his words, of "melancholy, incomparable beauty."[63] Although Malraux did actually produce and edit a new trilogy of art books, his *Musée imaginaire* nevertheless directly points to the library as an alternative space for experimental curatorial practice because it is here that the absence of artworks transforms into a different form of presence: in the form of their images—as well as their various relationships.

According to Rosalind Krauss, Benjamin and Malraux differed in their conception of originality. While for Benjamin a copy always impinges on an original with destructive consequences for its aura, in Malraux's estimation, photography yields a radical transformation of an object, thereby allowing for a new and different auratic charge. In language similar to Forster's description of Warburg, Krauss writes, "the imaginary museum was filled with a continued, though transformed, condition of aura. Which is to say that the imaginary museum was filled with 'meaning'."[64] In Malraux's case, this new charge consisted of the emergence of a transcendentally recognizable "style" based on the "premise ... that each work of art contains a potential for dialogue,"[65] that is, a dialogue among the works themselves and with their respective viewers. Regardless of the

63   Benjamin, "The Work of Art in the Age of Mechanical Reproduction," 226.
64   Rosalind Krauss, "The Ministry of Fate," 1002.
65   Jacqueline Machabéïs, "From East to West and Beyond," in *André Malraux: Across Boundaries*, ed. Geoffrey T. Harris (Amsterdam: Rodopi, 2000), 197.

have been more active in promoting open access is, at least partly, because when you've done your interpretation of Henry James and it doesn't come out for three years with a university press, nobody will die. But, if people are waiting for the results of your cancer research, it's a rather different matter. There is also a different set of sensibilities, research funding agendas, and expectations in science, and there is a more explicitly articulated need for research to be shared. Many scientists are simply being pragmatic with this, yet they have become quite radical through their pragmatism. And, obviously a lot of people in the humanities have taken on this pragmatism—and its successes—and are really trying to challenge the hegemony of big publishing corporations such as Elsevier or Springer in their search for alternative publishing models. Our interest with the *Living Books* project therefore lay in the politics of knowledge, but also in thinking across disciplinary boundaries. Personally, I've always been interested in biotechnology and bioethics. So, all of this science material I was reading and curating for my own living book on bioethics was useful to me intellectually, but I was also aware that involvement in the project allowed many humanities scholars to both consider science-related issues and reflect on the wider practices of knowledge production.

The *Living Books* project was partly inspired by Gary Hall's research into the idea of the book. With it, we wanted to challenge the notion of the book as a closed object, and to show that the book has always actually been open. Shakespeare's *First Folio*, for example, contained several hundred different typefaces. The book was therefore inherently unstable; it only became stabilized in a particular period of modernity, with the rise of liberal notions of copyright and authorship.

With this exploration, we were drawing on Gary's book, aptly titled *Digitize this Book!*[2] (That book came out as a traditional printed object from the University of Minnesota Press, which was a way to indicate that we should not just replace print with digital, or that everyone should publish everything open access, no matter what the circumstances.) Indeed, the aim of the *Living Books* experiment was to suggest that we need to focus on building horizontal alliances between different publishing institutions and different forms of publication. So, with this project, we also wanted to explore how we can open up this whole idea of life as a problem not just for humanities scholars to *think about*, but also to *live through*. Many scholars are very good at analyzing and writing about life, but not necessarily at reflecting on their own scholarly practices. So we were asking, what would happen if you tried to do both? *Living Books About Life* was therefore about taking this double agenda on board, but at the same time it was also quite modest. Its aim was just to signal what was possible, and show that, perhaps, things could open up a little bit.

E T
It is a kind of minimal provocation to say to humanities' scholars: "just try."

J Z
I think that's a good way of putting it: just try. And that's how we started a number of our projects, such as *Photomediations Machine*, which is an online site curated by myself and Taiwanese artist Ting Ting Cheng for work that deals with photography and other media. It showcases established photographers, artists, and social media work, as well as interesting scholarly and non-academic writing about this concept of "photomediation."[3] It also

various personal and academic attacks against him, what distinguishes Malraux's project and makes it especially considerable in light of contemporary discussions of the curatorial is his strong authorial and creative position in collecting, assembling, dis-assembling, and re-assembling visual montages. The *Musée imaginaire* is only possible because Malraux synthesizes his research, artistic intuition, and a curatorial agenda through precocious editing and design.[66] In the end, his trilogy is less an objective, scientifically sound analysis of figures and forms than it is a boldly composed fictional construction of, with, and through art and images. It is the aesthetic act of assemblage and juxtaposition, of making and displaying constellations in a post-Duchampian visual economy, that is the primary force for new meaning and for an overall technique that actually privileges the curatorial beyond the artistic:

> The striking success of this montage in which all the elements are inter-locked in order to produce a meaning which goes further than the sum of its components is due to the fact that the three facets of the triptych are the emblematic variations of a triple chronology: that of the lived, of fiction and of art. At every moment in Malraux's work and life, the simultaneous presence of these three overlapping "movements" affects his itinerary and validates his choices.[67]

66 While he does not bring up the notion of the curator, Grasskamp, in emphasizing the collective production process of the books involving a range of professionals (from photographers to museum curators to typographers and copy-editors), compares Malraux's work to that of a movie director—a role that sometimes comes up in discussions about curatorial work. Grasskamp, *André Malraux und das imaginäre Museum: Die Weltkunst im Salon*, 78, with additional references.
67 Jacqueline Machabéïs, "From East to West and Beyond," 203.

points to the intrinsically dynamic and processual nature of photography. *Photomediations Machine* is a sister project to our open-access journal *Culture Machine*. When we started *Culture Machine*—well, it was actually started by Gary Hall and media culture scholar Dave Boothroyd in 1999, and then I joined two years later—we were one of the first open-access journals in cultural studies and cultural theory, alongside journals such as *C Theory* and *Postmodern Culture*. It seemed quite radical at the time. But now, in the humanities at least, everybody is editing open-access academic journals, so we feel that we've done it—it's been fifteen years! That is why we're trying to open up *Culture Machine* and shift its editorial center to Latin America—specifically, to Mexico, where we've established a number of collaborations over the years—and see what happens when it is "genetically modified" like this.

A S
Is that being done in Spanish or English?

J Z
It's going to be done in both. At the moment it's only in English. For our special fifteenth anniversary *quince-añera* issue, we reccived texts in Spanish that we've translated back.

A S
Why are they being translated into English if you want to move from Europe to South America?

J Z
Having it in two, or even more than two, languages is the next step for us. But we also need to face the question of the actual readership, as well as, more importantly, the question of labor, of who will do the translation and of how that will work, etc. We're trying to explore all these other possibilities while remaining aware of the colonial associations any such translation or transmigration gestures may inevitably carry. It's definitely not going to be a case of Europe dictating or inviting the so-called Other (who is of course never fully other) to the party, but rather of allowing the Other to take control. At the moment, we are still only at the bridge, seeing what's going to happen, so we don't really know yet.

E T
I think there are some important issues to take up about the proprietary implications of translation as well. How does the circulation of translated material encounter the legal and propriety structures of various geographies?

J Z
Translation is a very interesting topic. But I would respond to your question in a more roundabout way by focusing on text-image relationships as a sphere where translation really takes on a curatorial life. And that brings me back to a thought that I let drop earlier. The *Photomediations Machine* project deals and experiments with images, but also—via the planned editorship of *Photomediations: An Open Book*, which I'm working on with photographer and scholar Jonathan Shaw as part of the European Commission-funded Europeana Space project—with the form of the book. As you know, early scholarly manuscripts were illuminated; they were also hand-copied and thus also contained a number of changes, corrections, substitutions, and individual marks. But, what has happened to academic manuscripts, especially in the last fifty or sixty years, is that they have become very unified, taking on the form of basic, black-print-on-white-page book blocks. Many scholars in the humanities don't really care or even think about what their book looks like,

More than half a century later, Malraux's legacy can be traced along the contours of various institutions, despite the fact that he was by no means an institutional curator. For example, Kate Fowle, the Director-at-Large at Independent Curators International, has defined contemporary curatorial engagement as follows:

> It could be said that the role of the curator has shifted from a governing position that presides over taste and ideas to one that lies amongst art (or objects), space, and audience. The motivation is closer to the experimentation and inquiry of artists' practices than to the academic or bureaucratic journey of the traditional curator.[68]

These remarks especially resonate with the reconsideration of Malraux's alternative curatorial genealogy; never afraid of blurring the boundaries of genres or media, throughout his life Malraux creatively maintained an ambiguous relationship between the conventionally distinct real (i.e. "history") and the imaginary (i.e. "fiction"). It was this general openness towards transgression and transformation that allowed him to design and construct a virtual "museum without walls" that exemplifies Foucault's notion of the archive as "the general system of the formation and transformation of statements."[69]

68   Kate Fowle, "Who Cares? Understanding the Role of the Curator Today," in *Cautionary Tales: Critical Curating*, ed. Steven Rand and Heather Kouris (New York: apexart, 2007), 32.

69   Michel Foucault, *The Archaeology of Knowledge & The Discourse on Language*, trans. A.M. Sheridan Smith (New York: Pantheon Books, 1972), 130.

only about what it says. So, with many of our projects under discussion we wanted to think about the book as an object, as a containment of ideas, but also to reintroduce a certain visuality to the humanities—which involves more than just sticking images in the appendix. We were also trying to raise questions about the hierarchy of the visual and the textual. We were not postulating that everyone should be working with images now simply because that's the culture we live in, but we wanted to loosen things up, to see how this idea of object production—and knowledge production within the boundedness of the book—really emerges. So, some of our experiments have also to do with exploring the role of visuality and thinking about how you could apply the criterion of rigor, rather than just the aesthetic criterion of pleasure, to thinking about images.

A S

The relation between quality and rigor is quite important to us in the *intercalations* project. You suggested earlier that some books need to be more perfect than others. Can you explain what you meant? What is the difference between a book that needs to be perfect and the book that can just be "okay"?

J Z

To be honest, I think no book ever turns out "okay." When my first-ever academic monograph arrived at my house—it was based on my PhD dissertation but had been completely rewritten—I didn't open it for a year. This was partly based on my relation to the book and partly because I really knew that it wasn't perfect. None of them ever are. One of the things I've learned over time is to accept—and maybe this is something I've tried to do with *Minimal Ethics in the Anthropocene*—that imperfection is an inherent quality of any act of production. Obviously, my

desire will always disengage or come apart upon the arrival of the produced object; it's never going to come together at the level of the concept or philosophy or image, and learning to work with people, with myself, with concepts in light of that is key. Let's take seriously what Deleuze or Bergson have to say about temporality and duration, about the idea of the "cut," which I argue you see quite clearly in Bergson, but especially in Deleuze, with his notion of *coupage*. If you take that cutting gesture beyond cinematography and see it as a certain ethical resolution of an instability, the moment of the cut becomes the moment of a temporary stabilization. It's never perfect and you have to enact that cut. There's therefore a link between incision and decision. A cut cuts through and enacts a resolution. This notion also connects to Karen Barad's agential realism in some sense.[4] There is an ethical position to be taken. A lot of resolutions are of course not human; they're undertaken by other agents. But the moment the human enacts a cut, mobilizing whatever compromises their faculties of critical thinking or their affective relations demand, an object occurs.

E T

Is this not fundamentally an engineering epistemology? I think to argue that we need to parameterize our relationship to the world to work in it is a way of asking about an engineering epistemology.[5]

J Z

Well, yes. Yes and no. Yes, in the sense that pragmatically this is how it might work. But, I think the engineering mindset prioritizes the pragmatics of the solution and says, "Let's just suspend the bigger picture because we need to get it done." Whereas I think a philosophical mindset might not lose sight of the wider horizon, and might be able to give an account of that moment of

Original Sun Pictures: Institutionalization

What had been predicted in the 1930s and 1940s about the capacity of mechanical reproduction to *transform* the archive of art by challenging its foundations, including the pretenses of originality and "access to authorship,"[70] eventually led to a change in the status of photography itself. As with all so-called "new" media, entry into the canon of art is often delayed; photography was no exception. By the 1960s, however, it had finally taken root; partly as a means to escape the rigid confines of institutional art production, a new generation of artists began to experiment with dematerialized forms of art making. Independent art publishing also experienced a surge; many artists and even some curators displaced their exhibitions between the covers of books, producing radical gestures such as *Twentysix Gasoline Stations* (1963) by Ed Ruscha, Mel Bochner's *Working Drawings And Other Visible Things On Paper Not Necessarily Meant To Be Viewed As Art* (1966), and *The Xerox Book* (1968), initiated and curated by Seth Siegelaub. From another perspective, there was also Andy Warhol's *Interview Magazine*, founded in 1969, and his use of polaroids and silk screening to reproduce the icons of mass media and mass production in bright colors and large formats. Industrial printing and photography, together with the book and the magazine as alternative spaces, became new means to further the deterritorialization of art.[71]

70 Consider Benjamin's full statement in "The Work of Art in the Age of Mechanical Reproduction," albeit regarding letterpress print: "the distinction between author and public is about to lose its basic character. ... At any moment the reader is ready to turn into a writer. As expert, which he had to become willy-nilly in an extremely specialized work process, even if only in some minor respect, the reader gains access to authorship" (232).

71 By 1972 these ideas were popular enough to be presented by the BBC in John

zooming onto the detail, or of this kind of temporary stabilization.

A S

But this is exactly where there is a paralysis of scale.

J Z

I don't claim that philosophers have to be Philosopher Queens, that they have to occupy a special place in society because they supposedly have more to offer. In a way—again, this horizontal working together of different groups of people and materials is very instructive—we've learned from scientists about open access and we can learn from others about other forms of organizing and doing things. We can learn about disruption from other agents and activists. I'm aware that an engineer can probably live just fine without a philosopher while I probably couldn't live without engineering in the daily, pragmatic sense of planning things, or using electricity, or my computer.

At the same time, philosophy is a luxury for a relatively affluent society that can afford to allocate at least some of its time and money to the activity of thinking. I think it's an important luxury that needs to be fought for. And, obviously, none of us just sit around and think; we do a lot of fixing as well, although it is a different form of fixing. At the same time, I'm thinking about co-production. What would happen if we slightly loosened up the hierarchy of intellectual and practical alliances regarding how things are produced?

E T

There are important affinities between the bombastic and the earnest. For example, Robert Smithson, within the history of artistic production, moved promiscuously among materials, concepts, and various scales and registers, but, I would argue, he wasn't being "cool"

about it. That is, there was an earnest approach to the scale of the cosmos, and this was a philosophical position. I am curious to know how you relate curatorial and publishing practices to the work of philosophy; are you doing philosophy with non-traditional means or media?

J Z

That is why my book *Minimal Ethics in the Anthropocene* is partly an attempt to write differently and to say less—it is only about half the size of an academic monograph.[6] It also tries to be a bit more minimal in its use of references. It still has them and it nods toward things that it should acknowledge, but it tries to avoid a very extreme exegetical reading, not because there is no room for it any more, but because, with this particular project, I wanted to enact something different. The book also includes what I call a "visual track," or a visual essay, that is a series of photographs supposed to simulate something like Ansel Adams's landscape photographs, or other kinds of god's-eye or bird's-eye views of landscape. Yet it also aims to poke fun at this top-down perspective. You look at the images once and you're not sure; you look again and see that what you're actually seeing is just a plastic bag. My attempt to have this visual track and construct this series of landscapes, which I have called *Topia daedala* ("manufactured landscapes") was driven by a desire to raise questions about the role of plastic in the age of petrochemical urgency.

But, I don't really address questions about associated substances or fossils or fuels in great detail in the book, partly because others have raised them before me. One of the reasons I decided to write the book was because so much of the research by scientists and social scientists on climate change and fossil-fuel depletion has already been done.

The initially unclassifiable appearance of such works is illustrated autobiographically in the essay "The Museum's Old / The Library's New Subject," written by art historian Douglas Crimp in 1981. He describes being hired to research image material for a documentary about transit, whereupon he claims he found Ruscha's *Twentysix Gasoline Stations* in the transportation section of the New York Public Library (NYPL) because that was where, at the time, it best fit in the collection. Art collections had not yet been extended to include such books, which were as inexpensive as they were unclassifiable. In his critique of the relationship between modernism and postmodernism, and the eventual institutionalization of radical art into the museum and the market, Crimp writes:

> I know now that Ed Ruscha's books make no sense in relation to categories of art according to which art books are cataloged in the library, and that that is part of their achievement. The fact that there is nowhere within the present system of classification a place for *Twentysix Gasoline Stations* is an index of its radicalism with respect to established modes of thought. ... For Ruscha's photographic books have escaped the categories through which modernism is understood just as they have escaped the art museum, which arose simultaneously with that modernism and came to be its inevitable resting place.[72]

Berger's four-part TV production *Ways of Seeing*. The corresponding book was published that same year by Penguin Books and includes a series of visual essays composed of photographs and art historical reproductions.

72   Douglas Crimp, "The Museum's Old / The Library's New Subject," in *Visual Culture: The Reader*, ed. Jessica Evans and Stuart Hall (London: Sage, 2005), 221.

The information is out there and still relatively little has happened, as Naomi Klein has highlighted in her recent book, *This Changes Everything: Capitalism vs. The Climate*. I didn't want to add to this catalog. The one that exists is already shocking enough. So I was just trying to gain a different entry point into the story of climate change. We've tried shock and awe, so maybe the minimal approach can do something else. Of course, I'm not naïve enough to think that my story will be the one that works, but I don't believe in the major approach to the story any more.

A S

The collapse of our civilization and of our planet seems to have, somehow, become a trend for new spectacles, events, exhibitions, marathons, etc. I see more and more of this kind of impressionistic apocalypticism, which rehearses a vague sense of peril as a means to produce an extinction spectacle and thereby sell more cultural products. How do you avoid this in your work?

J Z

This kind of apocalypticism, which is no doubt more and more prevalent these days, is a certain form of depoliticized melancholia that articulates someone's privilege and gives meaningfulness to their detachment from the world—and also perhaps to their sense of vacuity. I always want to say in those cases: maybe it's because *your* job and what you're doing in life really *is* meaningless. In a larger sense, we are all doomed, but it's not really "doom," is it? It is more of an historical inevitability. By saying that we are all going to die I'm not revealing any secrets. We all know that—and we also know that we are going to become extinct at some point in the future. But this only signifies "doom" in a particular sort of narrative. It becomes an inevitability only when we call up a certain scale.

E T

If it is true that ninety-nine percent of all life on earth has become extinct, yes, we can admit that at this immense scale, death is inevitable. But, there is still the question of politics in the present tense, and in the immediate future. We—the humans—are not dead yet. This gives rise to a parallel question about ethics: is there an ethical imperative, in your estimation, to give imperatives? Does intellectual work require intellectuals to give imperatives?

J Z

Yes, I was thinking that maybe I should issue imperatives more often. Now that I've let the *Minimal Ethics* book out into the world, I've been pushed to think about it more. The book ends with these twenty-one theses, which may or may not offer something to others. I have suggested people read them as poetry, but obviously they're something else as well. I wrote those theses as a gift for the wedding of artists Annie Sprinkle and Beth Stevens. Actually, that's how the book started. It was a queer wedding, at which the two artists married Lake Kallavesi in northern Finland. They'd married other objects too before, like earth, rocks, and snow—and there's a certain playfulness to their practice that I like. As I've said, I'm not directly engaged in any kind of eco-activism, but I have a certain sympathy for the intellectual and creative generosity that Annie and Beth promote with their work. The wedding required a gift, so I offered up the theses that now round off the book. (Somebody recently described them as the *catechism*, to my horror!) But the last chapter proper is a chapter on politics that tries to address the problems or accusations—much as you do, Etienne, in your introduction to *Architecture in the Anthropocene*— surrounding the Anthropocene as a kind of "grand leveler."[7] This equivocation is,

Meanwhile, Ruscha's books have become rare collector's items that sell for several thousand Euros and—since well before the term "media art" was debated as antiquated—photography has advanced into a proper, canonical genre. But, to describe how photography was gradually re-assessed "ultimately to be housed in the museum,"[73] Crimp recounts another story. For Crimp, this story matters most regarding the shifting of photography's status; for the reader-as-exhibition-viewer, it serves as an extraordinary example of an unorthodox curatorial engagement with the repository of the library that not only produced new visions and meanings through research, selection, assemblage, and juxtaposition, but ultimately transformed the very structure of the institution itself. In 1977, in the manner of Benjamin's aforementioned "interpreter of fate," the young librarian Julia van Haaften "renewed the old world" of the NYPL. Subsequently she would be promoted to work for nearly thirty years as the Director and Curator of the newly established NYPL Photography Collection department, which was fully inaugurated by 1982.[74]

73 Ibid., 217.
74 Housed in the NYPL's main building at Fifth Avenue and 42nd Street, in the Stephen A. Schwarzman Building, the department is officially called The Miriam and Ira D. Wallach Division of Art, Prints and Photographs: Photography Collection. It was developed over several years following van Haaften's groundbreaking exhibition; steps in the process included the launching of the Photography Documentation Project in 1979 and an expansion of the research unit through additional funding gained in 1980. Today the collection comprises half a million photographs, including, according to an official description: "images made for commercial, industrial, and scientific application as well as images for the press and other print media, the vernacular of amateur snapshot photography and original works intended for exhibition and/or the art market. ... The department's reference collection includes more than 20,000 volumes on photographers and the history of photography, exhibition catalogs, annuals, biographical dictionaries, and resource guides" (www.nypl.org/locations /tid/36/node/62335). Since 2005, Stephen C. Pinson has been the NYPL's current Assistant Director and Curator of Photography. He followed van Haaften in the

125

on the one hand, depoliticizing; but, on the other hand, it has an element of justice to it: even the rich cannot escape extinction. To bring that framework to bear on global capitalism is the only way to show that capitalism will inevitably die. In this way, the Anthropocene thesis is almost a perfect culmination of Marxism. The world will become extinct, just like everything else. Not that we should all sit back and wait for this to happen, or to extinguish all hope for action in the near term, but I think to put this idea on the table, as a horizon, is very important. And, this horizon of horror ... I suppose I am interested in a sort of shock-and-awe narrative that is being developed around the Anthropocene. Not the one that Stephen Emmott offers in his book *Ten Billion*, for example, but I do think that Naomi Klein's recent intervention is important.[8] She shows the crazy rationale of the climate change deniers who don't actually deny climate change, but who promote denial because it is in their (economic) interest. So, that kind of horizon of the Anthropocene is significant because it changes the terms of the debate. Sometimes they tell you that if you picture a really powerful person on the toilet, you lose respect for them.

E T
The Anthropocene as humanity taking a shit?

J Z
Well, yes, and I think that is actually a really powerful image in terms of envisaging alternative political systems and programs. Minimal ethics could perhaps be seen as one such alternative. I don't think minimalism should be confused with quietism. Perhaps we should go back and do what we did before we became critical theorists, when we went to graduate school and became smart activists, but retain the

Anthropocene as our horizon ... maybe something will shift then.

A S
There is an ongoing debate, far from the discussions of the Anthropocene Working Group, about whether the geological periodization of the Anthropocene should, from a cultural or philosophical perspective, be described instead as the Manthropocene, the Cthulucene, the Capitalocene, the Eurocene, the #misanthropocene, or the Anthrobscene. In your estimation, is it too easy to pawn off the Anthropocene on capital? Is it perhaps an existential reality that exceeds capital?

J Z
One thing I've been trying to do with this particular book, but also with a previous article I wrote for Tom Cohen's book called "Bioethics Otherwise, or, How to Live with Machines, Humans and Other Animals," was precisely to ask how to return to the human after the posthumanist critique.[9] This shouldn't be seen as some kind of species nostalgia, or an attempt to rescue what we've lost, or to go back to the way things were. Rather, I was trying to think about who is putting forth the posthumanist discourse, who is articulating the problems, and what my role in all of this is. I am therefore interested in the return to the human and the human-specific practices of philosophizing, art making, and engineering, in the light of these questions. For me, it still makes sense to think about art as that which is produced by the human, despite the nonhuman element in me.

E T
But, even in the biological register of the human, the brain is not the human brain! The brain is an iterative, evolutionary process. I don't want to live as a pig

Employed as an art reference librarian after finishing college in 1968, van Haaften processed art catalogs in an environment where she was told that the Library "simply did not collect photographs."[75] Inspired by the exhibition *The Truthful Lens: A Survey of the Photographically Illustrated Books 1844–1914*, curated by Weston J. Naef at the Grolier Club in New York in 1975, in which several books loaned from the NYPL were displayed, van Haaften began to investigate the holdings of her workplace during her spare time for volumes containing original photographic prints. With the MoMA's unique Department of Photography founded in 1940, it should be noted that there was at least this one institution in Manhattan that had already included "photography as a form of artistic expression on an equal footing with the other arts,"[76] thus contributing to a certain climate that would eventually acknowledge photography as a properly artistic medium. Remembering, van Haaften says, "Back in early 1975 when I began looking for photographically illustrated books, my initial plan was to make a bibliography of what NYPL had."[77]

role and in 2010–11 he curated the anniversary exhibition, *Recollection: Thirty Years of Photography at the New York Public Library*, which referenced van Haaften's first two exhibitions, *Original Sun Pictures* and *96 Images: From Talbot to Stieglitz*, the first show she curated in the new framework, in 1981.

75 Julia van Haaften, "A Picture of Persistence: How a Photography Collection Was Born," *The Huffington Post*, 1 October 2010, www.huffingtonpost.com/the-new -york-public-library/a-picture-of-persistence_b_747187.html.

76 See Thomas Weski, "Beyond the Pleasure of a Flawless Narrative," in *Cultures of the Curatorial*, ed. Beatrice von Bismarck, Jörn Schafaff, and Thomas Weski (Berlin: Sternberg Press), 307–17. With a view to the MoMA, Weski critiques the role and history of photography in general, and the Department of Photography in particular, as examples of how traditional curating in large museums operates through compartmentalization and strict chronology. He ponders what an emancipation of such traditions (which he sees initiated through the employment of Klaus Biesenbach as new "curator-at-large") could look like in order to be productive.

77 Van Haaften, personal email to the author, 2 October 2014.

or a microbe or a compost pile. I think a return to the question of what constitutes the human, what commits the human to the human, is absolutely crucial. But, then, let's return again to the role of the book. Why are we still making books in the Anthropocene? What can these formats and media really do if we reformat them and update their commitments?[10]

J Z

We could ask the same question about the exhibition. The exhibition does not cancel out the importance of protest; but it is an event in itself, an encounter, and there's a horizontality related to this encounter because we don't know the outcome. My way of doing ethics is not about telling people how to live—I'm still trying to figure that out myself—but I'm also attempting to turn this figuring out into a task, rather than give ready-made answers. My interest is also in casting critical light on those who claim already to know, and to show that what gets held up as ethics is often either just morality or plain moralism, as evidenced, for example, in the work of Alain Badiou. Morality is bad enough because it already assumes so many prior values, although it does contribute to the building of societies and communities. However, morality can easily turn into moralism, as Wendy Brown explains, at which point moral convictions or passions are turned into political mania, obsession, and, ultimately, stasis. The interesting thing is that when Badiou criticizes ethics, he can only do it in a condescending, moralistic way. I show in *Minimal Ethics* how, in his own little book titled *Ethics,* he compares ethics to an old maid who's become the toast of the town, and then everyone wants a bite of her. When I read that for the first time, I had to wonder, didn't he have an editor? Or, at least, a friend to tell him that this is really not on? I mean, I know

he's quite old-school, belonging perhaps to a time when women were only seen as either lovers of French men or house maids, but now women are also presumably his colleagues and peers (although Badiou would no doubt call them sophists, because they only masquerade as "true philosophers").

E T

But aside from this moralism, or perhaps in opposition to it, can we return to the "cosmic medium" of the book?[11] How does the book connect, as a technology, to what we could call a philosophical practice?

J Z

Breaking up and opening up the book doesn't mean annihilating it. I think it's important to acknowledge that. Again, to return to what I was saying earlier, my experiments inscribe themselves in the tradition of scholarly collaboration, both theoretical and practical. Most of these experiments are not purely mine; they are shared with Open Humanities Press, and draw on the work of people like Janneka Adema (currently a Research Fellow in Digital Media at Coventry University), Gary Hall, and others. I have been learning the tropes and ways of hacking the book all along. However, I have to say that I have great respect for the book. I grew up with books and I wanted to become a person who wrote books. And once I became this person, I started hacking the book-as-object; I mean hacking the object as a way of repurposing it for my own use. At some point, the form itself beckoned me to do something with it. That is why, in a lot of the projects I've been involved in, including *Living Books About Life*, *Liquid Books*, or the current project *Photomediations*, the book still returns and is retained precisely to highlight its inherent instability, to put that on the table and maybe to get

And, "After exhausting Naef's file and the few published bibliographies and dealers' catalogs, I took to exploring the geographical sections of the stacks looking for wrinkled pages and warped bindings, evidence of the pasted-in nature of photographs in nineteenth-century books and, particularly, albums."[78] With the help and support of colleagues who noticed what she was doing, she was first invited by editor Will Coakley to publish her collected index as a traditional scholarly bibliography of more than 500 entries in the *Bulletin of the New York Public Library*, the NYPL's in-house journal.[79] The invitation to curate an exhibition—in fact, the Library's first ever major photography exhibition—was then extended to van Haaften as a result of this bibliography. Created exclusively from within the holdings of the NYPL, the exhibition *Original Sun Pictures* followed from this invitation and was carried out under the watch of the former head of Art and Architecture, Don Anderle.

In general, exhibitions are not uncommon for large, prestigious libraries. They are evidently embraced as a means to attract audiences and welcomed as a possibility to showcase their collections. Today, the NYPL hosts approximately fifteen parallel exhibitions throughout its various branches at any given time. The Bibliothèque national in France recently presented Guy Debord's archive through the exhibition *Guy Debord: Un art de la guerre* (2013), and the British Library in London frequently displays selected treasures from its vast collection. It is important to point out, however, that the majority of these

78 Van Haaften, "A Picture of Persistence: How a Photography Collection Was Born."
79 Van Haaften, "Original Sun Pictures: A Checklist of the New York Public Library's Holding of Early Works Illustrated with Photographs, 1844–1900," *The Bulletin of the New York Public Library* 80, no. 3 (Spring 1977): 355–415.

others to play with us. I'm not even saying "with me" because, as you know from your own curatorial work, it has to be collaborative work, which goes beyond the individualism—or the neo-liberalism—of the subject, the author, the proprietor. And, it is not an either/or. I put my name, Joanna Zylinska on a book, although sometimes I know it is the Other in me speaking. But there are other situations where there is a more elaborate collaboration among people. How do *you* see the book? And why the book in the first place? Do you care about preserving it? Do you want it dead? Fossilized? Do you want to see it as a monument? What do you want to achieve with *intercalations*?

A S

We are beginning with the tool as a technology of the imagination as a way to explore the library as a curatorial project in relation to concepts and intellection. We are trying to avoid the gimmick, or of tricking out the book as a gimmick that would pretend to be a substitute for thought. We are pushing the concept of the paginated mind as a means to reimagine the relations between research, discipline, and creativity. As Foucault says, "the imaginary is a phenomenon of the library."

J Z

I appreciate that very much; it is key to avoid gimmicks and not to shove things down people's throats when it comes to experimentation and innovation. This can push the innovation in the design more toward the conceptual. Maybe the experiment really is somewhere else, rather than simply in the book's layout and fonts?

A S

In that case, what about the internet as a site and a platform for *Photo-mediations*? What about the spillage and transition between the various media of the book?

J Z

Through *Photomediations*, we are playing with the idea of the platform and its boundaries. What is a platform that is always adding new stuff? When does it run out? Where are the margins? When is there too much? What happens to things that have fallen down to the bottom? How do we foreground this original openness and instability of the book that has never really disappeared? How can a book explode and play with itself? These are some of the things we are trying to address.

E T

I'd like to go back to the book as printed matter. When we see relationships between books as a kind of thought-practice, or when we ask the question of the book as the "good neighbor," these are not simply imperatives to think about the book differently, but also invitations to ask another question: how is it that we come to think creatively about situations that seem completely stratified? We see the library as a place of experimentation in a way that Henry Miller and Virginia Woolf (among so many others) experimented in this space by juxtaposing different materials to provoke their respective writing practices to make intensive connections. With respect to the book as a tech-nology of thought, what are your criteria for the book? Or, what is the horizon for the book as a successful enterprise for thought?

J Z

Success is probably not a good criterion, because that would assume a linearity that's not there in the production of a book. It is more about trying to enact things differently, or maybe bring to the foreground this intrinsic instability of exhibitions still function according to the traditional matrix of curating: they are compartmentalized by genre and chronology, and based upon the aura of rare acquisitions and strange ephemera, as found in collections ranging from Louis XIV's medals room (in the Bibliothèque national de France), to the world's largest collection documenting psychedelic drug culture (in the Julio Mario Santo Domingo Collection at Harvard University's Houghton Library), to artists' books and printed matter (at the MoMA Library, as a subset of the museum). These exhibitions often present fascinating content while retaining a conventional form; as such, they do very little to experiment with or activate the discourse around the curatorial itself. Regarding book-themed exhibitions, it is usually younger artists and the graphic-design scene that produce more challenging formats; yet, such exhibitions tend to occur in independent project spaces or in the context of art book fairs, not in libraries. These shows do, however, often stress the book as artifact and use innovative exhibition design as their most distinctive characteristic, and thereby remain at a distance to relevant curatorial concepts and strategies.[80]

80   Regarding engagements with "real" libraries, three recent art projects should be mentioned: two, like *Original Sun Pictures*, from New York and one from Chicago. *The Library Project* (2001) was an unsolicited intervention into the holdings of the Harold Washington Library in Chicago, the largest municipal public circulating library in the US, organized by Marc Fischer of Temporary Services. One-hundred specially-made artists' books were carefully and secretly added throughout the stacks by replicating the libraries own cataloging methods. Reflecting on the official channels of bureaucracy by subverting them, the project articulated a desire to participate meaningfully yet autonomously in the creation of a common, public archive. Built around the surprise find on the shelf, it highlights moments of chance, discovery, and immediacy. From October 2012 to June 2013 the library of the Goethe-Institut New York hosted *The End(s) of the Library*. In order to question the library's contemporary role and potential, particularly in light of digital culture, curator Jenny Jaskey employed the classic strategy of inviting a range of artists already working with and about the book to develop new works in response to the site of the library. Partly

the book in some practices so as to allow others to see and put to the test that instability—while also *not* saying that we should all make all our books available online and read them as hypertext, because that would date this whole concept. I still like print and paper. Some of my preferences and affinities are historical; I come from a particular period and a certain generation. I think we can allow for experimentation while also returning to the appreciation of a particular form—and of what it means at a particular moment in time.

1   Joanna Zylinska, *Minimal Ethics in the Anthropocene* (Ann Arbor: Open Humanities Press, 2014).

2   Gary Hall, *Digitize This Book! The Politics of New Media, or Why We Need Open Access Now* (Minneapolis: University of Minnesota Press, 2008).

3   See www.photomediationsmachine.net

4   Karen Barad, *Meeting the Universe Half-way: Quantum Physics and the Entanglement of Meaning and Matter* (Durham and London: Duke University Press, 2007).

5   For a re-reading of William C. Wimsatt's "piecewise approximations to reality" by way of an engineering epistemology, see Reza Negarestani, "The Labor of the Inhuman," in *#Accelerate: The Accelerationist Reader*, ed. Robin MacKay and Armen Avenessian (Falmouth: Urbanomic, 2014), 425–66.

6   Zylinska, *Minimal Ethics in the Anthropocene.*

7   See "Who Does the Earth Think It Is, Now?" in *Architecture in the Anthropocene*, ed. Etienne Turpin (Ann Arbor: Open Humanities Press, 2013), 3–10.

8   See Stephen Emmott, *10 Billion* (London: Penguin, 2013); and Naomi Klein, *This Changes Everything: Capitalism vs. The Climate* (New York: Simon & Schuster, 2014).

9   Joanna Zylinska, "Bioethics Otherwise, or, How to Live with Machines, Humans and Other Animals," in *Telemorphosis: Theory in the Era of Climate Change*, Vol. 1, ed. Tom Cohen (Ann Arbor: Open Humanities Press, 2012), 203–25.

10 On the notions of format and commitment within inhumanism, see Reza Negarestani, "The Labor of the Inhuman."

11 Sarah Kember and Joanna Zylinska, *Life after New Media: Mediation as a Vital Process* (Cambridge, MA: MIT Press, 2012).

Returning to van Haaften's debut exhibition, *Original Sun Pictures*, presented at the NYPL's main building at Fifth Avenue and 42nd Street in May to July 1977, it is essential to recall that this show was curated by a librarian, whose convictions shaped the convention and format. As the show literally grew out of a library catalog, and the bibliography she had initially researched, it effects an inversion of the traditional order. Through the process of questioning the way in which the Library holdings had hitherto been categorized and cataloged she developed her exhibition, working carefully to investigate the interiors of books as unique and unconsidered curatorial resources. With the books as her building blocks, she displayed not only the remarkable individual discoveries, but also constructed a new perspective onto the NYPL's vast collection itself, revealing a new portrait so perspicuous that it would lead to a reconsideration of the repository and provoke a lasting rearrangement of the holdings.

running at the same time, the exhibition *Subliming Vessel: The Drawings of Matthew Barney* opened in May 2012 at The Morgan Library & Museum on Madison Avenue. The exhibition centered around Matthew Barney's sketches in preparation for his *Cremaster* film cycle (1994–2002) but also included his earliest and latest drawings as well as other works on paper. Presented on the walls and in glass cases, the works were arranged to act as "storyboards," or narrative tableaus, composed retroactively and only for the duration of the exhibition as combinations engaging a broad selection of medieval picture books and modern paperbacks, postcards, prints, and unique artifacts from the library's own expansive collection.

Andrew Norman Wilson, *Mechanick dyalling: teaching any man, to draw a true sun-dyal on any given plane, however scituated – 60*, 2014. Courtesy of the artist.

Fantasies of the Library

This is how it should be done. Lodge yourself on a stratum, experiment with the opportunities it offers, find an advantageous place on it, find potential movements of deterritorialization, possible lines of flight, experience them, produce flow conjunctions here and there, try out continua of intensities segment by segment, have a small plot of new land at all times. It is through a meticulous relation with the strata that one succeeds in freeing lines of flight ...

— Gilles Deleuze & Félix Guattari, *A Thousand Plateaus*, 1980

Among the exemplary fantasies of the library, an especially consequential series of events unfolded in London in the early 1960s. Two book lovers, the playwright Joe Orton and his boyfriend Kenneth Halliwell, were each sentenced to six months in prison for "institutional violation." The charge followed from their repeated theft of library books, which they altered by replacing their cover illustrations with humorously surreal, often sexually explicit collages, as well as by pasting their own comical text passages over the books' blurbs. Once reformatted, the couple would secretly return the modified texts to the library shelves, where they would re-enter the normal borrowing process. Presented in 2014 at Artists Space in New York City as *The Defaced Library: Books of Kenneth Halliwell and Joe Orton*, the installation consisted of a wallpaper created from blown-up black-and-white police photos of the couple's bedsit-cum collage studio, itself densely covered from floor to ceiling with portrait reproductions torn from innumerable art books—a paginated living space swarming with a multitude of characters, not unlike Saint Anthony's own prodigious experience. As the appropriated library and its unsolicited curators encountered the force of the law, Orton and Halliwell's experience of the state apparatus must have been a nightmare, not least because homosexuality was still

Andrew Norman Wilson, *An Inquiry Into the Nature and Causes of the Wealth of Nations – 365*, 2014. Courtesy of the artist.

ostracized, and even legally prosecuted, in most Western European countries. The library, a space of potential social emancipation, failed to provide a transformative sanctuary for the two men. In a passage from 1960, Orton pondered the revolutionary potential of the book, writing that "it would vibrate the structure, but not enough."[81] The couple spent nearly three years constructing and dispatching their interventions, but the violence of the State proved inexorable. Not ten years after their imprisonment, Halliwell, who suffered from severe depression, tragically killed his partner Orton before committing suicide himself. Half a century later, the books they modified are considered valuable artifacts, with a special place in the collection of the Islington Local History Center, London.[82] The commemoration of these interventionist works within such a collection evokes a strange affect; indeed, the institutional absorption of a revolutionary gesture is no matter of celebration for those still committed to vibrating the structure by repurposing its function.

This account of so-called institutional violations evokes the tragedy of two other men who also lived together and shared a tenacious affection for the library: François Denys Bartholomée Bouvard and Juste Romain Cyrille Pécuchet. As the main characters of Flaubert's last book, *Bouvard et Pécuchet*, published posthumously in 1881, the two copy-clerks arc consumed by their desire for scientific knowledge. As clerks, however, the pair have no particular training in

81   A passage including this sentence from Orton's *The Vision of Gombold Proval* (1960) was used as the epigraph for the didactic panel of the display on Orton and Halliwell's story presented in the exhibition *The Library Vaccine*, Artists Space, New York City, 25 September–16 November 2014.

82   Some images of the cover interventions can be found here: http://joeorton.org /Pages/Joe_Orton_Gallery13.html.

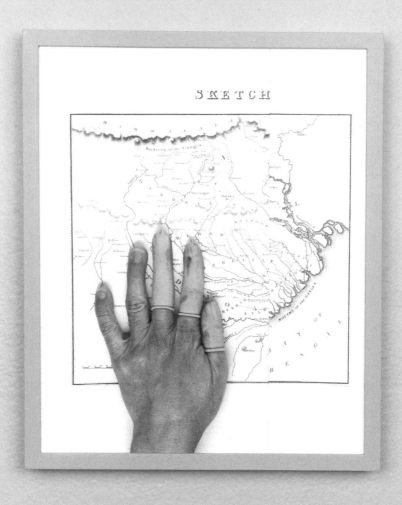

Andrew Norman Wilson, *A Picturesque Tour Along the Rivers Ganges and Jumna, in India – frontispiece*, 2012. Courtesy of the artist.

evaluating anything beyond reproduction; yet, once they are freed from the constraints of tiresome labor and have retired to the countryside, they are seized by the characteristically (for Flaubert, at least) modern lust to explore and absorb all knowledge. Relying on their professional background of directly copying texts, Bouvard and Pécuchet thus acquire and consult an encyclopedic range of scientific books covering agriculture and animal husbandry, medicine and anatomy, chemistry, astronomy, geology, history, archaeology, and many other disciplines, which operate as analogic models for their own naïve actions within the narrative. Perversely immune to perceiving the creative relationship between experience and knowledge, every new project Bouvard and Pécuchet undertake goes farcically wrong; every experiment is botched; every dish spoiled; every design a disgrace. Every time they set out to present their newest achievement to a public of neighbors and distant friends, they inspire only aversion, shock, disbelief, and scorn. Yet they are stubbornly modern, that is, unable to learn from previous mistakes, hurrying instead to take up ever more grotesque tasks to heap on their ever-growing pile of failed emendations. They are a twin emblem of the unintended consequences of dispassionate interest, oscillating as they do between tragedy and farce in an arms race of epistemic reductionism. A menacing caricature of the modern scientific mentality, Flaubert's novel is no less a manifesto for the forms-of-life in perpetual excess of empirical observation, the accumulation of texts, or the sequencing of information. With each new failure of Bouvard and Pécuchet, we are reminded that the library's power is not as a container of knowledge, but lies instead, in the words of Alberto Manguel, "in the experience rescued from the page and transformed again into

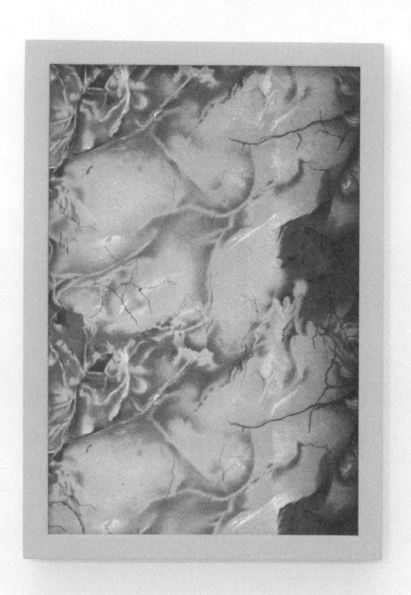

Andrew Norman Wilson, *The Encyclopedia Americana* – 879, 2014. Courtesy of the artist.

experience, in the words reflected both in the outside world and in the reader's own being."[83] According to translator Mark Polizzotti in his introduction to the Dalkey Archive Press English edition of *Bouvard et Pécuchet*, Flaubert "unearthed a darker truth of scientific progress, one as yet largely unsuspected, and in our century all to familiar: that experimental dispassion so easily shades into depraved indifference."[84] While in *La Tentation de saint Antoine* the act of reading explodes into a firework of associations and constellational mutations with a force that Foucault described as "magic power," the clerks' reading remains uninspired, as any meaningful integration of that crucial spark is denied by the modern firewall of universalized dispassion. Although they are "directly tempted by books," they cannot transcend "the grey expanse of the library."[85] The fantasies of exactitude and totality that preoccupy Bouvard and Pécuchet are the same ones that confine them to the banality of merely confirming and accumulating observations. Of course, thought demands careful observation and rigorous discipline, but these alone do not provide the requisite potency for creative construction; it is only when observation and discipline are invigorated by the promiscuous adjacencies and kaleidoscopic entanglements of anexact relations that the imagination is produced. This process is, by definition, interminable. As Flaubert knew well, "Ineptitude consists in wanting to conclude."[86]

"To admit authorities," Virginia Woolf writes, "however heavily furred and gowned, into our libraries and let them tell

83   Manguel, *The Library at Night*, 91.
84   Mark Polizzotti, "Stan and Ollie in the Lab," introduction to *Bouvard et Pécuchet*,
      by Gustave Flaubert (Urbana-Champaign, IL: Dalkey Archive Press, 2005), xv.
85   Foucault, "Fantasia of the Library," 106.
86   Polizzotti, "Stan and Ollie in the Lab," xxxiii.

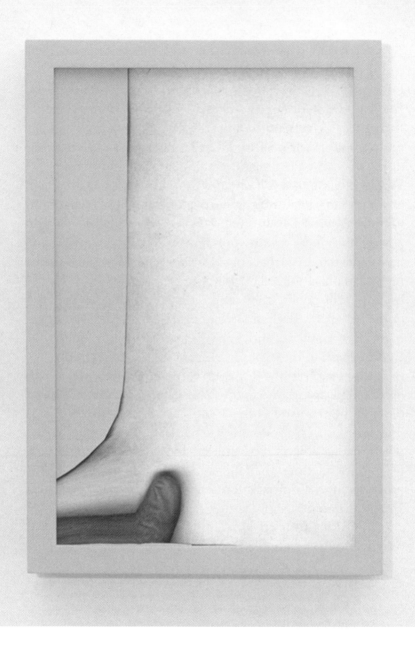

Andrew Norman Wilson, *The Economic Review – 5*, 2014. Courtesy of the artist.

us how to read, what to read, what value to place upon what we read, is to destroy the spirit of freedom which is the breath of those sanctuaries. Everywhere else we may be bound by laws and conventions—there we have none."[87] Taken together, the cases of Orton and Halliwell and *Bouvard and Pécuchet* remind us that the curator of the library is tasked with relaying this spirit of freedom described by Woolf. Fantasies, in this constellation, are neither a product of fancy nor of spontaneity, but result from the passionate and careful treatment of the library as a curatorial space. Because of this, and despite Foucault's remark to the contrary, the reader-as-exhibition-viewer should never leave it to the police or the bureaucrats to see that the library is in order.[88]

I am thankful to my professors Beatrice von Bismarck, Thomas Weski, and Benjamin Meyer-Krahmer, under whose guidance I developed a first draft of this essay as my thesis in Curatorial Studies at the Hochschule für Grafik und Buchkunst Leipzig. I moreover feel grateful to Charles Stankievech for the dedicated conceptual support during the early version of this essay, especially when discussing the concept of melancholy with regards to the library. Thanks also to Antonia von Schöning for initially pointing me to André Malraux; to Leah Whitman-Salkin for the ongoing exchange about all things books and libraries; to Julia van Haaften for the correspondence; to Etienne Turpin for his editorial precision and ceaseless enthusiasm in my research, ideas, and our collaborative experimentation, learning, and unlearning; as well as to Michael Levine for generously inviting me as the 2014 Craig-Kade Scholar in Residence at Rutgers University, which gave me a space to focus on this book as well as the *intercalations: paginated exhibition* series as a whole.

87   Virginia Woolf, "How Should One Read a Book?" in *The Common Reader: Second Series*, http://gutenberg.net.au/ebooks03/0301251h.html#e26.

88   Original sentence by Foucault: "Do not ask who I am and do not ask me to remain the same: leave it to our bureaucrats and our police to see that our papers are in order. At least spare us their morality when we write." In *The Archaeology of Knowledge & The Discourse of Language*, 19.

Contributors

ERIN KISSANE is co-founder of *Contents* magazine, the editor of *Source*, a resource for code and interactive design in newsrooms, and director of content for *Source*'s publisher, Knight-Mozilla OpenNews. Before joining OpenNews, Erin was editorial director at Happy Cog Studios and an independent web-publishing nerd in New York and Portland. She lives in Brooklyn with her partner and their daughter.

HAMMAD NASAR is a curator, writer, and (since 2012) Head of Research and Programmes at Asia Art Archive, Hong Kong. Formerly based in London, Hammad co-founded the non-profit arts organization Green Cardamom. He has curated or co-curated numerous international exhibitions, including: *Lines of Control: Partition as a Productive Space*, Johnson Museum, Cornell University, Ithaca, NY (2012) and Nasher Museum, Duke University, Durham, NC (2013); *Beyond the Page: The Miniature as Attitude in Contemporary Art from Pakistan,* Pacific Asia Museum, Pasadena, CA (2010); *Where Three Dreams Cross: 150 Years of Photography from India, Pakistan and Bangladesh*, Whitechapel Gallery, London, and Fotomuseum Winterthur (2010); *In the Milieu of Fatah Halepoto*, Sindh Museum, Hyderabad, and VM Art Gallery, Karachi (2010); *Safavids Revisited*, British Museum, London (2009); and *Karkhana: A Contemporary Collaboration*, Aldrich Contemporary Art Museum, Ridgefield, CT (2005), and Asian Art Museum, San Francisco, CA (2006). Most of these projects were accompanied by symposia and book-length publications. Hammad was a Fellow of the UK's Clore Leadership Programme and a Research Fellow at Goldsmiths College, London. He plays an advisory role for a number of arts organizations internationally, including the Delfina Foundation (UK) and the Rhode Island School of Design (USA).

MEGAN SHAW PRELINGER is a writer, artist, and naturalist. She is the author of *Another Science Fiction: Advertising the Space Race 1957–1962* (2010), and the forthcoming *Inside the Machine: Art and Invention in the Age of Electronics* (due from W.W. Norton in 2015). Both books are part of her study of the relationship between art and technology in the twentieth century, research she has lectured on to American and international audiences. She is currently an artist-in-residence at the Exploratorium. She is also co-founder, with Rick Prelinger, of the Prelinger Library, and is the designer of the library's geospatial arrangement system. Her work has been profiled in *The New York Times*, *Harper's*, and *Make: Technology on Your Time*. She also leads urban naturalist walks with San Francisco Nature Education.

RICK PRELINGER is an archivist, writer, and filmmaker. His collection of 60,000 ephemeral films was acquired by the Library of Congress in 2002. Beginning in 2000, he partnered with Internet Archive to make 6,500 films available online for free viewing, downloading, and reuse. His archival feature *Panorama Ephemera* (2004) played in venues around the world, and his latest feature project *No More Road Trips?* (2013) received a Creative Capital grant in 2012. His *Lost Landscapes* projects have played to many thousands of viewers in San Francisco, Detroit, Oakland,

Los Angeles, and elsewhere. He is a board member of Internet Archive and frequently writes and speaks on the future of archives and issues relating to archival access and regeneration. With Megan Shaw Prelinger, he also co-founded the Prelinger Library in 2004. He is currently Associate Professor of Film & Digital Media at University of California, Santa Cruz.

ANNA-SOPHIE SPRINGER is a curator, writer, and the co-director of K. Verlag in Berlin. Her practice merges curatorial, editorial, and artistic commitments by stimulating fluid relations among images, artifacts, and texts in order to produce new geographical, physical, and cognitive proximities, often in relation to historical archives and the book-as-exhibition. Her previous projects as curator include the series *EX LIBRIS* (2013) on how to make exhibitions out of books and libraries at Hochschule für Grafik und Buch-kunst Leipzig; Galerie Wien Lukatsch, Berlin; and Arg.org. Her most recent exhibition, *125,660 Specimens of Natural History* (2015), was co-curated with Etienne Turpin at Komunitas Salihara in Jakarta, Indonesia, in partnership with the Indonesian Insti-tute of Science. As a member of the SYNAPSE International Curators' Network of the Haus der Kulturen der Welt, she is the co-founder and co-editor of the *intercalations: paginated exhibition* series published as part of Das Anthropozän-Projekt. Anna-Sophie received her M.A. in Contem-porary Art Theory from Goldsmiths College, University of London, and her M.A. in Curatorial Studies from the HGB, Leipzig. In 2014 she was the Craig-Kade Visiting Scholar-in-Residence at Rutgers University. She is currently researching her Ph.D. on the financial-ization of nature and a new form of natural history exhibition in times of ecological collapse at the Centre for Research Architecture at Goldsmiths.

CHARLES STANKIEVECH is an artist whose research has explored the notion of "fieldwork" in the embedded landscape, the military industrial complex, and geopolitics. His diverse body of work has been shown interna-tionally at institutions including the Louisiana Museum of Modern Art, Humlebaek, Denmark; Palais de Tokyo, Paris; Haus der Kulturen der Welt, Berlin; Thyssen-Bornemisza Art Contemporary, Vienna; MASS MoCA, North Adams; Musée d'art contempo-rain de Montréal; Canadian Centre for Architecture, Montreal; and the Venice and SITE Santa Fe Biennales, among others. He has lectured at dOCUMENTA (13) and the 8th Berlin Biennale for Contemporary Art; his writing has been published by Sternberg, *e-flux Journal,* The MIT Press and Princeton Architectural Press. Charles has participated in such residencies as The Banff Centre, Marfa Fieldwork, Atlantic Centre for the Arts, Museumsquartier Vienna, and the Canadian Military. His comprehensively researched curatorial projects include *Magnetic Norths* and *CounterIntelli-gence*—both critically acclaimed as the top Canadian exhibitions of 2010 and 2014, respectively. In 2015, he won the OAAG award for best solo exhibition with *Monument as Ruin*. He is an Editor of *Afterall Journal* out of London, and since 2011, he has been co-director of the publishing project K. Verlag in Berlin/Toronto with Anna-Sophie Springer. In 2007, he was a founding faculty member of the Yukon School of Visual Arts in Dawson City, Canada—a partnership with the indigenous sovereign nation of Tr'ondëk Hwëch'in. Charles is currently Director of Visual

Studies in the Faculty of Architecture, Landscape, and Design at the University of Toronto.

KATHARINA TAUER is a German graphic designer currently living and working in Berlin. After completing her M.A. in Art Direction with a focus on type design at ECAL (École cantonale d'art de Lausanne) in 2012, she moved to London and built up a solid, year-long work experience at Zak Group. Katharina now works on self-initiated projects, as well as commissions and freelance jobs, maintaining a focus on book design and the cultural sphere.

ETIENNE TURPIN is a philosopher researching, designing, curating, and writing about complex urban systems, the political economies of data and infrastructure, art and visual culture, and Southeast Asian colonial-scientific history. He is a Research Scientist with the Urban Risk Lab at the Massachusetts Institute of Technology, a Visiting Research Fellow at NTU CCA Singapore, founding coordinator of the Urban Lab Network Asia, and founding director of anexact office in Jakarta, Indonesia. He is the co-editor of *Art in the Anthropocene* (Open Humanities Press, 2015) and *Jakarta: Architecture + Adaptation* (Universitas Indonesia Press, 2013), and editor of *Architecture in the Anthropocene* (Open Humanities Press, 2013). As a member of the SYNAPSE International Curators' Network of the Haus der Kulturen der Welt, he is the co-founder and co-editor, with Anna-Sophie Springer, of the *intercalations: paginated exhibition* series within the framework of Das Anthropozän-Projekt.

ANDREW NORMAN WILSON is an artist based in New York. His work has exhibited at MoMA PS1, New York; Centre Pompidou, Paris; Palais de Tokyo, Paris; Ullens Center for Contemporary Art, Beijing; CCS Bard, Anandale-on-Hudson; The Hammer Museum, Los Angeles; Project Native Informant, London; Fluxia, Milan; Yvon Lambert, Paris; New York Film Festival; the San Francisco International Film Festival; and, the Images Festival. He has lectured at Oxford University, Harvard University, Universität der Künste Berlin, and CalArts. His work has been featured in *Aperture, Art in America, Artforum, BuzzFeed, Frieze, Gizmodo/Gawker, Kaleidoscope, The New Yorker,* and *Wired.*

JOANNA ZYLINSKA is Professor of New Media and Communications at Goldsmiths, University of London. The author of five books—including *Minimal Ethics for the Anthropocene* (Ann Arbor: Open Humanities Press, 2014), *Life after New Media: Mediation as a Vital Process* (with Sarah Kember; Cambridge, MA: MIT Press, 2012), and *Bioethics in the Age of New Media* (Cambridge, MA: MIT Press, 2009)—she is also a translator of Stanisław Lem's major philosophical treatise, *Summa Technologiae* (Minneapolis: University of Minnesota Press, 2013). Together with Clare Birchall, Gary Hall, and Open Humanities Press, she runs the JISC-funded project *Living Books About Life,* which publishes open-access books at the crossroads of the humanities and the sciences. Joanna is one of the editors of *Culture Machine,* an international open-access journal of culture and theory, and a curator of its sister project, *Photomediations Machine.* She combines her philosophical writings and curatorial work with photographic art practice.

Fantasies of the Library

Co-editors
Anna-Sophie Springer
& Etienne Turpin

Designer
Katharina Tauer

Copy Editors
Lucas A.J. Freeman
& Jeffrey Malecki

Editorial Assistants
Miriam Greiter
Martin Hager
& Louis Steven

Printing and Binding
in the United States of America

This edition © 2016 Massachusetts
Institute of Technology

Published by
The MIT Press
Cambridge, Massachusetts
02142

ISBN 978-0-262-03520-0

This book is a revised, second edition of
intercalations 1: Fantasies of the Library,
edited by Anna-Sophie Springer and Etienne
Turpin (Berlin: Haus der Kulturen der Welt and
K. Verlag, 2015). The original edition of the
book was published in association with Kirsten
Einfeldt and Daniela Wolf as the opening
volume of the *intercalations: paginated exhibition* series, a publication project of SYNAPSE—
The International Curators' Network at the
Haus der Kulturen der Welt, Berlin. This series
is made possible by the Schering Stiftung; it
appears in conjunction with "The Anthropocene
Project 2013/2014," an initiative of Haus der
Kulturen der Welt, Berlin, in cooperation with
the Max-Planck-Gesellschaft, Deutsches
Museum, Munich, the Rachel Carson Center
for the Environment and Society, Munich,
and the Institute for Advanced Sustainability
Studies, Potsdam.

Haus der Kulturen is funded by:

The book was made possible by:

And produced by:

K. Verlag, Berlin
http://k-verlag.com

Anna-Sophie Springer's work on this volume
was generously supported through the Fall 2014
Charlotte M. Craig Visiting Research Scholar
and the Max Kade Writer/Scholar in Residence
Program in the Department of German
at Rutgers University, New Brunswick, NJ.